The COMFORTING PRESENCE *of* GOD

NANCIE CARMICHAEL

HARVEST HOUSE PUBLISHERS

EUGENE, OREGON

Cover by Left Coast Design, Portland, Oregon

Cover photo © Peter Adams/Photographer's Choice/Getty Images

THE COMFORTING PRESENCE OF GOD
Copyright © 2004 by Nancie Carmichael
Published by Harvest House Publishers
Eugene, Oregon 97402
www.harvesthousepublishers.com

Library of Congress Cataloging-in-Publication Data

Carmichael, Nancie.
The comforting presence of God / Nancie Carmichael.
   p. cm.
ISBN 0-7369-1429-3 (pbk.)
1. Christian life.   2. Presence of God—Meditations.   I. Title.
BV4501.3.C38 2004
242—dc22   2004001425

Printed in the United States of America

04 05 06 07 08 09 10 11 / DP-MS / 10 9 8 7 6 5 4 3 2 1

Acknowledgments

Thanks to my friend Betsy West—first a reader of my columns and now a dear friend—for her initial encouragement to put these devotions in a book. To my prayer group—you know who you are—thank you for your incredible prayer support. Prayer does make a difference!

Most of all, thank you, my amazing husband, Bill; my wonderful children and grandchildren: Jon, Brittni, Will, Kendsy, and Cali; Eric and Carly; Christian and Jami; Andy; and Amy. You light up my life, and I love you more than I can say!

Contents

Inviting Him into Our Lives

*I, even I, am He who comforts you.
Who are you that you should be
afraid?*

Isaiah 51:12

Sometimes change can be scary. There are many unknowns, and we are not given a preview of what's ahead. We may have hints or clues, but life just unfolds before us. But in all of the changes I am aware there is something else I can count on: God's Word and His unfailing, comforting presence. *No matter what.* We are not left alone on this journey, even when it seems like it.

As I look back over the last 20 years of writing magazine columns out of the experiences of my life, one thing that stands out is the inevitability of change. When I began writing for *Virtue* magazine, all five of our children were at home, and Bill and I were up to our necks in school, sports, church, and magazine work.

As of two weeks ago, our last chickadee flew the nest and we became empty-nesters. We now work from our home in the writing, speaking, and publishing field. After our daughter, Amy, drove out of the driveway, I have to admit Bill and I high-fived each other and then climbed into the hot tub. (Okay, she moved only 20 miles away, and now she's back home for a few days...but still, it's another transition.) I guess I've learned that the good-byes that were so wrenching weren't final—they just reflected change. Our children do come back—bringing fiancées, sweethearts, wives. And now children! Last year our second-oldest son, Eric, married Carly in a joyous family celebration. And in March of this year our son Jon and his wife, Brittni, welcomed their third child, Cali Pearson. Then, in September, our son Christian married his sweetheart, Jami, and they are off on life's adventures. And there are more changes in the wind—good ones, which promise blessings.

At this time in my life I am humbled by all I have been given—my husband and children, my life experiences, my wonderful friends and extended family. And yet I have never been so aware of my brokenness and inadequacy. There is wisdom in maturity, but even in the wisdom there is an increased sense of knowing what I *should* do versus what I *do* do. Or should have done versus actually did do. But I have learned to welcome the broken places because, as Oscar Wilde wrote, "How else but through a broken heart may Lord Christ enter in?"

What have I learned in the past 20 years? Winston Churchill once said, "The farther backward you look, the farther forward you are likely to see." It's important to look back because doing so helps us understand the future. As I look back, I see that fads come and go—but balanced truth from God's Word endures. I've learned, too, that none of us are exempt from life even if we do it all "right"—and I've learned it's impossible to do it all "right"! I've also learned it's important to give grace to others because, sooner or later, we'll need grace ourselves.

Perhaps most importantly, I've learned that in a changing world I can cling to an unchanging God. Jesus is the same—yesterday, today, and forever. His Word—faithful and true—never changes. I am more convinced than ever that we need not be afraid of facing our most perplexing and desperate needs, because when we cry out to Him from those places, He meets us and restores us through His life-giving Word. We all suffer some kind of disappointment or loss, and although there is an enemy who actively seeks to destroy, a stronger truth is, "Greater is he that is in [us], than he that is in the world" (1 John 4:4 KJV).

Also, I've learned to look ahead—not dwell on the past. Paul the apostle wrote, "One thing I do: Forgetting what is behind and straining toward what is ahead, I press on" (Philippians 3:13-14 NIV). What's ahead for all of us? It can be tempting to be content where we are. But without vision, the people perish. Through changing seasons, I've found that *I must put myself in a place to increase my vision.* Sometimes vision is thrust upon us, but there are times we must actively seek new vision, waiting on God to show us, and praying, *"God, what will You have me do?"* In this, most importantly, we can examine our own hearts and lives and be honest about the needs that touch us most deeply.

Both of my parents were wonderful mentors to me, although they were not perfect by any means. I realize my magazine columns often reflect what I learned from watching their lives. They are both gone now, but their lives still instruct me.

Though this year I have seen many good changes in my own life, the other day I was wishing I could have a heart-to-heart chat with my mother. How did she navigate the waters of change? How did she keep growing in her walk with God?

I dug out Mother's journal and looked for entries she made when she was the age I am now. Her seven children were growing and changing, as are mine. My father had cancer, and she did, too. Yet she recorded this: "So much has happened! As I've read back over my diary, I am impressed with this truth: *God will keep!* Through it all, He will keep. In it all, He will keep. Praise His name!"

As I read back over my own writings and journals, I agree with my mother. He does keep us, and He comforts us with the knowledge that He will never leave us nor forsake us. My prayer and deepest wish for you is that, as you read through these devotions, you will reflect upon your own life and invite Him in, no holds barred. We can agree with the psalmist's prayer from thousands of years ago:

> *Your unfailing love, O LORD, supported me.*
> *When doubts filled my mind, your comfort gave me*
> *renewed hope and cheer…The LORD is my fortress;*
> *my God is a mighty rock where I can hide.*

PSALM 94:18-19,22 NLT

1

The Everlasting Arms of Grace

*We do not have a High Priest who cannot sympa-
thize with our weaknesses, but was in all points
tempted as we are, yet without sin. Let us therefore come boldly to the throne of grace, that we may
obtain mercy and find grace to help in time of need.*

HEBREWS 4:15-16

Bill and I were leaving to go on a weekend speaking engagement. The final details were almost complete, but Amy, our then six-year-old daughter, began acting up. She jumped up and down on my bed, deliberately scattering things I had laid out for the trip. I sternly corrected her, but as I went into the kitchen to serve dinner, she followed me, grabbed her place setting off the table, and put it back on the counter. Her little face was a storm cloud. I was about to lose my patience, when I realized something was troubling her deeply.

I got down on the floor where she was sitting, took her in my arms, and looked into her dark eyes. "Amy," I said softly, "what is wrong?"

She threw her arms around me and burst into sobs. "Don't leave me, Mommy! Please don't leave me!"

My heart broke for her. I understood how vulnerable she felt at the idea of being "left." She had been abandoned as a baby and spent the first three years of her life in a Korean orphanage. My love seemed so inadequate to fill the deep emotional hole that an abandoned child is left with. I felt helpless, not knowing what to offer except my assurances...*again.* How could I convince her, how could I make her *know* I would never abandon her, that I would come back? I got down with her and took her in my arms, not able to help my own tears.

Suddenly Amy stopped sniffling and looked up at me, surprised. "Hey—why are *you* crying?"

"Amy, I feel sad because you are sad. But I promise you I will never stop being your mother, and I love you, always."

"Oh Mommy, I love you, too!" She kissed me exuberantly and jumped up and ran off to play, all smiles. And there I sat on the floor, wondering what that had all been about!

I think I know. When Amy was honest with me about her fears, my tears and my loving arms showed her that I identified with what she was feeling. They also showed that I loved and accepted her just as she was. Her expression of vulnerability and need did not make me love her any less. When she realized that someone understood how she felt, she experienced immense relief. That was a healing moment in her life because it was another step on the path toward a growing assurance that she was wanted and loved.

We all long to be understood, to know that someone cares how we feel. The experience with Amy reminded me that our beautiful High Priest, Jesus, literally "got down" where we lived, became human, and therefore understands our feelings. His nail-scarred hands prove His love for us. He longs for us to know that He cares, that we can run to Him in our weakness and humanness, and that He will always be there, loving and accepting us.

It is His plan, His design, that we accept His love and, in turn, offer it to others. But how do we do that? Jesus knows the truth about us, and still He loves and accepts us when we truly come to Him. If we are to be understood by others, we must risk facing—and telling—the truth about ourselves.

Some time ago, two friends and I were having tea and discussing what the body of Christ really means—how we need to tell each other the truth and truly listen to and care for one another. One of my friends said, "I feel for you, Nancie, because some people put you on a pedestal. That must be hard."

That was my opening to tell my "real" truth. I took a deep breath. "Well, frankly, I'm not doing very well. My pride keeps me insisting, 'I can handle this, I'll solve it,' but I can't." Then I promptly broke down and cried. My friends put their arms around me and prayed for me. Their arms, their prayers said enough. When they left to go home, my burden was lighter. My laughter was real and my smile genuine. What a wonderful thing it is to be loved, imperfections and all!

Amy received healing because she was able to articulate her deep fears to someone who cared. I received healing as I confessed to my friends I didn't have it all together. James 5:16 says, "Confess your [faults] to one another, and pray for one another, that you may be healed."

Our transient, busy lives make it difficult to find safe places to confess our needs. We struggle with some common misconceptions: "If I'm honest about the way I feel, she won't want to be friends with me." Or, "I was vulnerable once and she betrayed my confidence, so—never again." Further, it can be costly to truly listen to another's pain because often there isn't an easy solution. Real listening can make you feel helpless.

Out of that experience with Amy and the later one of having tea with my friends, I learned that to experience true healing, I must tell the truth. I also realized I can be part of others' healing by having the courage to respond to the honest feelings they express. Once I have done that, I can pray for them more fervently.

What about you? Do you know God's unconditional love and grace? Have you felt God's arms around you through the loving acceptance another person has shown you?

Now think about someone who may need *you* to be God's arms of understanding and love. Is it one of your children? Is it your spouse? Is it a co-worker or neighbor or friend? Ask God to allow you to be the extension of His everlasting arms to someone today.

Prayer

    Lord, I know You want us to *know* Your love...to experience it deep in our hearts. Help us to truly receive Your grace by allowing You into those places where we are most weak and vulnerable—where we need Your cleansing and healing.

    Give us the courage to be open with others—to receive Your love and grace from them as we see and speak the truth about ourselves. And then, Lord, to offer healing and grace to others by offering them our presence and our prayers. In Christ's name, amen.

"In agape love there can be no pride. For by its very nature it produces humility...We take it as recipients of grace. We become little children and...empty our hands of all our striving, all our goodness, all our works— we receive the gift of God. And when that grace of God enters our hearts it is so unmerited, so overwhelmingly gracious, that it sends us to our knees in deepest gratitude."

—E. Stanley Jones, *Christian Maturity*

2

A Fresh View of Praise

Oh, that men would give thanks to the LORD for His goodness, and for His wonderful works to the children of men! For He satisfies the longing soul, and fills the hungry soul with goodness.

PSALM 107:8-9

One late February afternoon I'd been working long and hard at my computer and needed to get out of the house. Although we live near the mountains, we cannot see them from our house because we're surrounded by trees. To see the mountains, I must walk to the meadow. I was not only tired of the weather, my life itself seemed dreary— stagnant and boring—almost as if someone had hit the "pause" button. I was at a plateau. The travel section in the Sunday paper was filled with descriptions of exotic, faraway places that sounded wonderful. I was ready to see a new view of life, a new country. But today a trip to the meadow would have to do.

I put on my jacket and gloves and tromped through the trees, hurrying before it got dark. The air held just the hint of a thaw, and I heard the sound of an early red-winged blackbird. Before long I reached the meadow, and sure enough, there were the mountains. I stopped and caught my breath. The still, breathtakingly blue sky was spectacular, with the sun setting on the great billowing clouds and the mountains. The brilliant colors of purple and silver and white were like the palette of an exotic artist.

I paused and simply took in the view. *Thank You,* I breathed. *Thank You.* How wonderful it was to savor His world, His presence. I thought of the psalmist's description: *"Clouds and darkness surround Him; righteousness and justice are the foundation of His throne...The heavens declare His righteousness, and all the peoples see His glory"* (Psalm 97:2,6). As is my habit when I walk, I pray. I automatically began to pray again for a need that had been bothering me for some time—but then I stopped.

This time, instead of pleading and petitioning God as I usually did, I began to praise Him for His perfect answer. And my petty discontent and concerns seemed to fade in His presence and in the light of His magnificent creation. Suddenly the birds, which had seemed quite incidental before my walk, now seemed the important thing, and I was amazed to see tiny buds on a willow tree. I was reminded of Jesus' words: "Look at the birds of the air...your heavenly Father feeds them. Are you not of more value than they?" (Matthew 6:26). As I slowly walked through the meadow, I was aware my depression had lifted. What had changed? Nothing—and everything. My life had the same needs, the same situation—yet it was new because, as I held it up to Him in praise, I was in a new place.

Genesis 29:31-35 tells the story of Leah, wife of Jacob. She was sure if she bore Jacob sons, he would love her, but he didn't. He loved Rachel instead. What a sad, dreary place for someone to be—unloved and unwanted. Finally, after the birth of her fourth son, Leah said, "Now I will praise the Lord." Her situation hadn't changed, because Jacob still did not love her, and yet it had—because of the dynamic of praise. Leah made up her mind that she would praise God from where she was, and she had a fruitful life. Learning to praise Him in all things is a dynamic that is changing my life. I wish it hadn't taken me so long to learn this incredible secret, but the concept of living continually in a spirit of praise and worship can seem as far away as a Caribbean island. It sounds wonderful, but how do I get there from here?

It is one thing to go to church, to sing the praise songs...but it is another to *live* with an attitude of praise and worship. I've found that it's simple and yet profound. Deuteronomy 30:14 says, "The word is very near you, in your mouth and in your heart." Praise comes from an honest heart of obedience, a recognition of God's powerful presence, and faith that He cares for me. Not that everything is always hunky-dory. It is, after all, a *sacrifice* of praise that we bring. He is worthy of my praise because, if there is anything I know about Him, it is that He is the Redeemer—He redeems all things. And He is faithful. How can we *not* praise Him? Yes, often I do withhold my praise, waiting for some magic moment. But when I simply make up my mind to praise Him, I get a fresh perspective, I see the big picture of life regardless of circumstances.

Choosing to live a life of praise is like being in a wonderful new place. Praise is a new way of thinking, of speaking. How wonderful to know that we can be in the midst of life *with Him* as praise continually fills our hearts and minds and mouths. "I will bless the LORD at all times," David sang. "His praise shall continually be in my mouth" (Psalm 34:1). Try this: Read Psalms 103 and 104, and from those psalms, list things for which you can praise the Lord. Fill your life with praise—by singing in the car, or by humming a worship song to Him, or simply by saying "Thank You!" to God by your attitude. Look around you...see the sky and God's creation. Read Psalm 96 and praise God *with* His creation.

Prayer
Lord, it is Your will that we praise You, continually and in all things. Help us not to wait for the "right moment" or withhold the praise that You so deserve. You are a good God, and You give us all things—from the very air we breathe to the food we eat. May we cultivate a spirit of praise toward You always: in difficult times, in good times, in times of joy, and in times of frustration. Lord, open our eyes to see the blessings You give, that we may praise You for Your goodness to us. In Jesus' name, amen.

Praise to the Lord,
O let all that is in me adore Him!

All that hath life and breath
Come now with praises before Him.
Let the Amen
Sound from His people again:
Gladly for aye we adore Him.

—JOACHIM NEANDER

3

Persistent Faith

I cried out to God with my voice—
to God with my voice; and He gave
ear to me.

Psalm 77:1

I was in my small group Bible study and we were sharing prayer requests. My friend asked, "Nancie, what can we pray about for you this week?" Well, I knew very well what my number-one heart cry and need was—it was personal, and it was for my daughter. But I'd given that prayer request so many times that when it was time to open my mouth I instead asked prayer for a relative who was having health problems. Why didn't I tell my most urgent need? Because I was thinking, *Here I am with the same old prayer request. Again. I'm sure my friends are tired of hearing it.*

The truth was, I was tired of it. How many times had I approached God, asking for the same person, the same chronic need? And yes, God had answered, God had intervened in miraculous ways in the past. But sometimes a situation seems so chronic and complicated that it feels fruitless to keep asking. It seems to me that the deepest prayer needs—the ones most personal and nearest to my heart—are never clear-cut. They often feel urgent, ongoing, messy, and inconclusive. Sometimes they are so personal I can't even articulate them—I just pray them to God. And yes, I have seen wonderful, amazing answers. But often the same person is back on my list. *Again.* Sometimes there's nothing to write in the *answers* column in my prayer journal...other than *waiting.*

It's hard to keep praying, keep asking for a breakthrough, when it looks as if nothing is happening. I'm tempted to think, *Maybe God just isn't going to answer that prayer, so why keep on about it?* It can be too discouraging and too wearying. How do I keep praying, keep believing in the face of what seems to be a stone wall? What's the point? It's less emotionally taxing to pray for the needs of others not so close to me. It's easier to say to my friend about her situation, "Don't give up—just believe God."

When I got home from Bible study that day, I did some studying on what it means to pray. There is a clear pattern in Scripture. Often the people who came to Jesus with desperate needs were mothers, fathers, or close friends. Sometimes they came to Him with their own needs. There was the persistent widow who had a legal problem (Luke 18). There was the father who hadn't gotten any answers for his epileptic son (Luke 9). There was the group of friends who cut a hole in a rooftop to lower their sick friend down in front of Jesus (Mark 2).

These desperate, determined, and persistent people who received answers from God had no other place to go. They also went out of their way to get answers—they pursued Him, went to where He was. They were stubborn in their faith—and they wouldn't give up, because they knew Jesus was their only answer, their only hope. Some of them were shameless in their pursuit of Him— yet they didn't care. They hung onto God, whether with little or great faith, knowing He would provide…and He did. Their faith was rewarded.

I was especially taken by the story of the Canaanite mother who had a demon-possessed daughter (see Matthew 15:22-28). She wouldn't let Jesus alone until He heard her and healed her daughter. The story captivates me because it shows incredible faith. Jesus had His hands full with the people He was trying to reach, and the woman was an annoyance to the disciples, who wanted just to get rid of her. Verse 23 says that Jesus did not answer a word to her, in spite of her pleading. And yet *even in His silence* she worshiped Him. Her faith was irresistible to Jesus, and He exclaimed, "O woman, great is your faith! Let it be to you as you desire" (verse 28).

Do we worship Him, even in His silences? Like the persistent mother in Scripture, I come to Him again and again in prayer, persistently believing He is my only hope. Reading God's Word has helped build my faith, and faith says, *Hold on. Believe what seems impossible. He is able, He is faithful. He cannot deny Himself.*

Do you have a chronic need that sometimes you are weary of praying about? We can pray with persistence because God's love for us is persistent, and He never stops reaching for us. His ways are not our ways, His thoughts are not our thoughts, and His Holy Spirit is working in ways we do not see.

Prayer

Lord, I praise You for Your intimate knowledge of our needs. Father, it seems as if some of our deepest prayer needs are the ones that are most chronic—the ones we return to and pray for over and over. I pray that You will teach us what it means to have persistent faith—to continue to seek Your face, knowing that it is not Your will that any should perish. We praise You for the answers! In Jesus' name, amen.

Let nothing trouble or sadden you,
All passes, but God does not change,
You will conquer all with patience;
You lack nothing if God is in your heart,
His love is enough.
—TERESA OF AVILA

4

Trust God, the Great Remodeler

If indeed you have heard Him and have been taught by Him...be renewed in the spirit of your mind, and...put on the new man which was created according to God, in righteousness and true holiness.

EPHESIANS 4:21,23-24

We've had many special moments in our 25 years of marriage, but this was not one of them. I was ready to throw the wallpaper tray right at my beloved. We were in the upstairs bathroom on one final leg of our remodeling project, trying to paper a room that was not square. When I'd ordered the paper months before, the blue seashell theme and border had been attractive. Now it wasn't coming together, and I thought if I ever saw a blue seashell again it would be too soon.

What a mess. Remodeling had seemed like a great idea months before, when Bill and I had walked through each room, dreaming what we could do. The "cozy" look we had liked 12 years before, with dark beams and wood paneling, had felt dingy and oppressive. We had needed change—we had wanted *light.*

And now, struggling with the wallpaper, I was feeling like my house: very much *used*. God was reminding me that I needed renewal. How like Him to speak to me through even this. *Funny,* I thought, *how you can live with something for a long time and not realize that God is actively shaping you, working on changes.* As if I were trying to paper a wall that wasn't square, I was getting the message that something basic was wrong. God was using chronic physical pain to get my attention. Finally, Bill and I decided on thorough medical testing.

After several days of tests, the doctor strode into the examining room with my chart. "Neurologically, organically, you look healthy," he said. "We could call what you have 'fibromyalgia,' but I believe a lot of your symptoms are caused or exacerbated by stress. Can you cut some things out of your life?"

We discussed treatment, stress management, physical therapy, and pain medication, but my mind was whirling. *Stress! Who* doesn't *have stress these days?* On the way home, the question haunted me: *Why do I—a follower of Christ—have so much stress that I hurt?*

Something was wrong here. Early in life, I'd learned that good performance equals acceptance with God and man—and I'd learned the lesson well. The doctor's words echoed in my mind: *"Do you have to do so much? Who do you think you are, Wonder Woman?"*

After one of the tests, a spinal tap, I'd had to lie flat for two hours, alone, covered with a blanket. The months of pain and frustration had culminated there, leaving me helpless and angry.

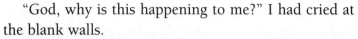

"God, why is this happening to me?" I had cried at the blank walls.

In that silence, I began to sense the presence of God, to hear His voice: *Come unto me, you who are soul-weary. Come, my yoke is easy, my burden is light. I will give you rest.* I began to realize in my helpless condition, *This is how I really am before Him. None of my accomplishments brings acceptance. What I do must be an outgrowth of a relationship, not the main event.*

It was one of those moments in life that was a wake-up call, and I wanted to "get it"—not ignore it. I knew God was clearly saying to me, "Trust My grace."

I didn't throw the wallpaper tray that day, and ultimately, we finished our remodeling. But it took longer and was a bigger mess than expected (we had to call in the experts several times). And life didn't stop in the process. I remember moving Sheetrock one evening in order to climb into bed! But we kept going, knowing the end result would be wonderful.

So it is with "remodeling" a life. Sometimes our worn-out creeds (such as working to earn grace) need to go, but it takes persistence and vision of what's possible. It takes an understanding where we want to change, how it will look. Of course, maintaining a life is also an ongoing process, just as is maintaining a house. I must revisit my priorities periodically in order to keep fresh— to keep my life relevant and vital.

Perhaps you sense that your own life is in need of remodeling. Just as you know when you live in a house for a while and it's not "working," you sense that your life is not "working." Try this: List five values you believe that you "live." Are some of these values, consciously or otherwise, not God's best for you? Are they perhaps causing some problems in your life? How can you re-order your life in order to walk in newness and freshness?

Prayer

Father, I freely admit I need Your wisdom to re-order my life. Show me how to let go of things that need to go. May I learn to tell the truth in love, to recognize my own weaknesses that need Your forgiveness. May I learn as well to celebrate the gifts that You have given me. Give me courage to say "no" when I should in order to say "yes" to the important things, so that my life will honor You. In Christ's name, amen.

"Grace...can make you strong enough and brave enough to take off your superself mask and begin to look at your real self. For it's your real self which God loves and for which Christ died, your real self with all its sins and flaws which He has always known and never stopped loving. Feeling this at gut level gives you courage to face yourself as you truly are."

—David Seamands, *Healing Grace*

5

He's Big Enough

Don't worry about anything; instead, pray about everything. Tell God what you need, and thank him for all he has done. If you do this, you will experience God's peace, which is far more wonderful than the human mind can understand. His peace will guard your hearts and minds as you live in Christ Jesus.

PHILIPPIANS 4:6-7 NLT

The year I was 16, the world began to open to me in wonderful ways. But at the same time, I was becoming aware of the ugly, confusing side. I'd learned with growing horror of the Holocaust. The civil rights movement was in full swing, making me aware of injustice in my own country. And worst of all, Vietnam's tragedy reached our farming community: Our neighbor's son was killed there. The God I loved and had pledged to serve with all my heart seemed far removed, especially when one Sunday evening I heard my pastor preach (directly to my sister and me) on the evils of makeup. It didn't make sense. What kind of God did I have anyway?

One night after supper, Mother and I were doing the dishes. We had our best talks as she washed and I dried. The debate inside of me was reaching a boiling point, and I felt I'd die if I couldn't unburden myself. Mother was my safest choice, but I wasn't certain of her reaction.

"Mom—" I blurted, my heart pounding. "I've been thinking. I don't believe there is a God. It all seems like a cruel joke."

Mother wiped her hands on a dish towel and laughed a little as she pushed a strand of auburn hair back from her face. She looked at me, her brown eyes gentle: "Of course God is there, Nancie. And it's okay that you're thinking. What good is anything if you can't question it?" Her eyes were keen with amusement and tenderness. "He's always been there for me, and He'll always be there for you," she said confidently. "Now let's get these dishes done."

Later, I wondered why—*Why didn't Mother tell me I was going to hell? Why didn't she wring her hands at the thought of her daughter rejecting the faith? What made her so sure there was a God?* The fact that she had laughed had completely disarmed me and somehow brought immeasurable relief even though I didn't fully understand what had happened. I only knew that her response was pivotal in my life.

Years after this, I found a letter Mother wrote concerning a tragic, bittersweet time in her life before she became a Christian. (Even after she became a Christian, she rarely discussed that period of her life because she said it was so painful.) She wrote, "It is in the past—God has forgiven me and He has forgotten. And I *try*...but God has assured me that 'His grace would be sufficient.' And it is."

Is, not *was*. That was how she knew for sure about God. Her faith didn't become strong in one blinding moment. It grew in the daily walk through God's Word, through His persistent love that never let her go, through good times and bad. Often during my childhood, I remember, Mother would grab her Bible, get in the car, and say, "I'm going to pray for a while—I'll be back in half an hour," and she would drive off down the lane to an isolated spot. It was her secret weapon...one available to us all.

Mother's response to my questions that day at the kitchen sink was important because it mirrored God's response to all of us. God is big enough to handle our doubts and fears. He's not threatened by our honesty— instead, He reassures us, *Of course I'm here—I'll always be here for you. Trust Me and see.*

Prayer
    Lord, how good it is to belong to You—even though it is a walk of faith, and sometimes we don't see so clearly. Thank You, Lord, for helping us to grow, even in our doubts and questions. How wonderful it is to trust Your never-failing love that keeps us in all our ways. In Jesus' name, amen.

"In the dark days of the Reformation in Europe, Luther wrote to a friend: 'I am against those worrying cares which are taking the heart out of you. Why make God a liar in not believing His wonderful promises, when He commands us to be of good cheer, and cast all our care upon Him, for He will sustain us? Do you think He throws such words to the winds? What more can the devil do than slay us? Christ has died for sin once for all, but for righteousness He will not die but live and reign. Why then worry, seeing He is at the helm? He who has been our Father will also be the Father of our children.'"

—Alfred E. Cooke, *Treasury of the Christian Faith*

6

The Life God Uses

*Then I heard the Lord asking, "Whom should I send
as a messenger to my people? Who will go for us?"
And I said, "Lord, I'll go! Send me."*

ISAIAH 6:8 NLT

It was 1967, and Bill and I were newly married. He was
a youth pastor as well as being in graduate school. I
worked full-time, helping him the best I could. Life was
hectic. One evening when we were at a gathering with
several other couples, the leader of the group turned to
me and said, "Nancie, why don't you share what God is
doing in your life?" I gulped, my face turning red. I hated
the word "share"; it seemed so overused. Besides, it didn't
seem as though God was doing anything in my life. But
I knew Christian "lingo," and managed to rattle off something phony. Later the question burned inside of me: *How
do you get something to share?*

Lately I've been considering what it means to really
"share" from my life. Maybe because by the time this is
in print, I'll be a grandmother for the first time. But
somehow it seems urgent that I give God full permission

to use me any way He will. I believe He's calling me to be a leader, to share (there's that word again) from my life. A leader is anyone with influence, so actually all of us are leaders of some kind.

When I was a senior in high school, I received a scholarship from a local service group for leadership. I gave a short speech at their meeting, but I felt like an impostor. *Me—a leader?* I privately scoffed. I struggled with organization and being up front. I still do. I tend to think there are enough voices clamoring to be heard, people wanting to be at the front of the pack—why should I jump into the fray? It's easier for me to take potshots at the world from my deck, stay cloistered in my Christian community, and have a good time working in my garden. But I can't get away from the fact that I have been given much…How can I *not* share? I am learning these important principles on how to let God use my life:

I must be willing. When God called Moses to leave the land of Midian and go back to lead His people out of Egypt, Moses didn't have confidence in his own abilities. He begged God to use someone else. But he began to tentatively follow God, and over time God made him a great leader. Before the prophet Isaiah could share God's truth, he had to come to a place of humility and submission. Then he said to God, "Lord, I'll go. Send me."

I must have faith in something bigger than I am. Moses was able to carry out his task because he got his directive from God. He kept his eye on the big picture. Earlier, when he had intervened in a fight between two Israelite slaves, they had not welcomed his input with open arms.

"Who made you a ruler over us?" they had demanded. If people responded to me the way the Israelites did to Moses, I would burst into tears and resign! But Moses kept listening to God. What holds me up is belief in God's Son, Jesus Christ, and in the fact that the Bible is God's Word, relevant for today.

I must seek out mentors. Moses gained knowledge growing up in the Egyptian courts, and practical wisdom from his father-in-law, Jethro. Seeking out mentors for different times and challenges is an ongoing process. Quiet time with God and His Word mentors me. My parents, my husband, and many special people have built their influence into my life. Thought-provoking books by ancient and contemporary authors mentor me. And now I find myself being mentored in surprising new ways by my growing-up children.

I must not allow failure to keep me from sharing. Passionate commitment to something bigger than I am helps me not be defeated by my own inevitable mistakes. Failures can be embarrassing, humiliating, hard on my pride. But with God's forgiveness and mercy, I can go on so that failure does not define my life. It is amazing to think God can use me, mistakes and all. As I look back at the few times when I think God really used me, I am humbled to see that it was in spite of myself. True sharing comes out of what God has given us.

Disappointments only refine the message. Recently, after a disappointment related to sharing, I said, "Never again! Forget speaking. Forget being a leader. What do I have to say, anyway? Let somebody else do it who can do it better." It's true that someone else could do it—God's work doesn't hinge on me. *But I would be missing out.* And God uses disappointments to help refine His message in my life.

Ask yourself this: *Am I willing for God to use me where I am? What do I have to share with others out of the difficulties I've experienced?* Remember, God tests and purifies His message in the lives of the people He chooses to use. And it is in the testing, the painful trials, that God makes Himself real to us. When you allow God's grace fully into your disappointments and failures, He will give you an honest and strong message that you can share with others.

Prayer

Lord, You have given us so much. We are like clay in Your hands. Continue to mold and shape us into Your image, so that even the painful experiences become monuments to Your mighty provision. I pray that we will be generous people, giving people, who are willing to share with others from the abundance of what You have brought into our lives. And as we do, may others be drawn to You. In Jesus' name, amen.

"The one who has had but little trouble in life is not a particularly helpful person. But one who has gone through a hundred and one trials, experiences, deaths, blasted hopes, shocks, and a tragedy or two and has learned his lesson...such a person is worth while. He is able to enter into the need of suffering humanity and pray

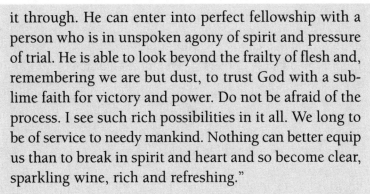

it through. He can enter into perfect fellowship with a person who is in unspoken agony of spirit and pressure of trial. He is able to look beyond the frailty of flesh and, remembering we are but dust, to trust God with a sublime faith for victory and power. Do not be afraid of the process. I see such rich possibilities in it all. We long to be of service to needy mankind. Nothing can better equip us than to break in spirit and heart and so become clear, sparkling wine, rich and refreshing."

—J.W. Follette, *Broken Bread*

7

Knowing His Voice

*The sheep hear his voice; and he calls his own
sheep by name and leads them out. And when he
brings out his own sheep, he goes before them; and
the sheep follow him, for they know his voice.*

JOHN 10:3-4

I look out our laundry room window onto our two
springer spaniels' doghouse and their little fenced yard.
They see me and leap up—adoring, worshipful, wagging
their tails. Since I hardly ever get adoring, worshipful
looks while I'm in the laundry room, I weaken. *Okay,
guys...*I put on my jacket and go out to them, leashes
in hand. "Let's go for a romp." We walk toward a meadow
where they can run freely.

The earth has a musky, warm smell to it, and red-
winged blackbirds, like exotic ornaments, bob on the
limbs of willow trees. A chipmunk darts across our path,
and Walter bolts, nearly pulling me over. "Hey—wait until
we get to the meadow!" I know if I let them off the leashes
today while we are still in the neighborhood, there will
be trouble. Especially with Norman, who is prone to
wander. Oh, he comes back, but he always takes the long

way, and often is deaf to my calls. Then he returns—innocent, smiling, asking how I am.

These are not my dogs, you understand. They're our son's, but since dogs don't go to college, and neither do I, here we are—Norman, Walter, and I. We reach the meadow and crawl under the barbed-wire fence, and I let the dogs go. Off they bound, ears flopping as they run over logs, following their noses, going crazy with all the tantalizing scents.

I follow them to the edge of the meadow, sit on the grass, and lean against a tree, basking in the sun and the quiet beauty of the meadow. I am glad for this moment of peace, to leave the house, the phone, people...my people—wonderful as they are.

As I look off in the distance toward the snow-covered mountains, I think back to an afternoon more than 22 years ago. A nondescript day, really, but I vividly recall that as I bathed and fed our toddler and infant sons, I prayed, *Lord, help me always say "yes" to You. Regardless of where You place me, of how my life unfolds.*

I didn't fully understand what I was pledging to God then. And I haven't always said "yes" to Him. There have been times when I haven't wanted to listen because I wanted my own way. Like Norman, my heart is prone to wander. But I did know I wanted to know Him better, and I wanted to grow.

I hear a voice calling in the distance, and I look to see a woman standing on the other side of the meadow, walking her dog. As she calls to her dog, Norman and Walter run toward her. I stand and yell at them, calling them back. Finally they wheel around, realizing where I am. They come back to me and drop by my side, panting. "You silly things," I scold. "Don't you know my voice?"

Do you know My voice? It was one of those quiet moments when I knew God was talking to me. Outwardly it would seem that not much has changed with me— same husband, same family, all growing older through the natural progressions of life.

And yet now, I have an inner hunger that cries, *I'm not satisfied with the status quo! I want to take the next step...to live for God as never before.* I don't want to just "cope," to make it through life to heaven, safe at last. But how do I grow?

Growth is much easier to measure when we look at visible, tangible things we can measure: opportunities, success, education. And yet our Lord says, *"Sitting at my feet, getting to know Me—this is the good part, the part that will never be taken away"* (see Luke 10:42).

On our walks in the winter when the snow is deep, the dogs stay close to me. But springtime? Watch out! During the hard, stormy times of my life, I hold fast to my Good Shepherd's hand. When the sunny meadow of life is sweet, though, I develop an illusion of my own strength. That is when I must know His voice as never before.

Know Him as my Source, not just a resource. Grow in the fruit of the Spirit in my home, where I'm known best, following Him right where I live. Does Jesus have more of me now than He did 22 years ago? Do I know

His voice so intimately that I am quick to respond? Living in obedience to His Word—as George Mueller said, on "my knees"—that's how we get to know His voice. He does speak; He has not left us comfortless or alone. All He asks is that we keep our hearts turned toward Him, saying *"yes."*

Prayer

Lord, You call to us in Your still, small voice, saying "Come away, My beloved." In this hectic world, it can be hard to listen to You, to cultivate hearing Your voice. Thank you for reminding us that You are speaking. Give us the courage and discipline to listen to Your voice—to protect our relationship with You above all the distractions of life. And then, after hearing Your voice, may we have the courage to obey You. In Jesus' name, amen.

"God is speaking. Not God spoke, but God is speaking. He is, by His nature, continuously articulate. He fills the world with His speaking voice…If you would follow on to know the Lord, come at once to the open Bible expecting it to speak to you. Do not come with the notion that it is a thing which you may push around at your convenience. It is more than a thing, it is a voice, a word, the very Word of the living God."

—A.W. Tozer

8

Lessons Learned in Winter

*Be patient, brethren, until the coming of the Lord.
See how the farmer waits for the precious fruit of
the earth, waiting patiently for it until it receives
the early and latter rain. You also be patient.
Establish your hearts, for the coming of the Lord
is at hand.*

My words came back to haunt me: *"What we need is
a good, long, hard winter!"*

It had been a beautiful, late-fall Saturday when I'd said
that to Bill. We had taken our two dogs for an outing
off an old logging road up into the mountains and begun
hiking up a seldom-used trail. We had been alarmed to
see how dry everything was. Creek beds, springs, and
waterfalls stood empty. Dried moss on the rocks was mute
testimony to former days of plentiful rain and snowfall.
Little puffs of dust arose from our steps as we tried in
vain to find water for our dogs to drink. Fortunately, we'd
brought a jug of water with us, and as we sat in a grove
of pine trees and ate our lunch, we shared our water with
the dogs. That's when I'd turned to Bill and made my
smart remark about needing winter.

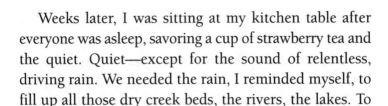

Weeks later, I was sitting at my kitchen table after everyone was asleep, savoring a cup of strawberry tea and the quiet. Quiet—except for the sound of relentless, driving rain. We needed the rain, I reminded myself, to fill up all those dry creek beds, the rivers, the lakes. To make a deep snowpack for the spring and summer.

I was going through some of my old journals. I read entries from different times in my life:

> Age 15: *I am so disgusted with myself! I can't get anything accomplished. I wanted to write today, do my homework, answer three letters, memorize a Chopin nocturne, study U.S. history. But all I got done was my choir work. And I don't think anybody even appreciates it!*

> College freshman: *I am sitting hopelessly in the middle of a mess. I'm tired and I'm still not ready for finals tomorrow. I promised a friend I'd type a paper for her, too. Help, I'm drowning!*

> Middle-aged mom: *Lord, here I am again, feeling angry, like Martha—"Why don't they help me? I'm doing it all on my own"—and anxious—"Can I get it all done?" I have a constant sense of suffocating pressure. Every minute is so crammed full.*

What else is new? I thought ruefully. I evaluated my "to do" list lying next to the stack of journals along with next year's calendar and gave a deep sigh. How many times in quiet moments like this would God persistently call to me, *"Be still...know that I am God...cease your striving"*? It seemed that I planned ahead so much that I didn't have time to be *here*…so much into the next season that I missed hearing what God was saying to me *now.*

The rain continued for days after that, and then it began to snow. The snow would stop for brief periods, then start again. We made lame jokes about putting up flags so we could find each other's houses. And then we had to pay people to shovel off our roofs so they wouldn't collapse. We had a good, hard winter all right—weeks, months of it. We had many cups of strawberry tea as we watched the snow pile up; many of our plans had to be canceled due to icy roads. I struggled against a sense of isolation—"cabin fever," some call it. But there was nothing to do but "let it snow," as my father used to say.

One afternoon I was trying to get ready to leave for a speaking engagement, yelling at the kids, "Pick up your things!" "Do your homework!" As I heard my voice, shrill with the Martha syndrome again, I decided to get out of the house, go for a walk. I prayed as I walked, *Lord, how difficult love is! I embark upon this quest of learning to love, learning to listen, but life intrudes on my good intentions. The people I love the most drive me crazy!* I walked in the stillness, in the coldness. It was almost dusk, and the air took on an alpenglow hue, the sky nearly blending into the snow in a pale pink. I walked, letting my frustration dissipate in the quiet. I meditated on these verses: *"Truly my soul silently waits for God…He leads me beside the still waters; He restores my soul…In returning and rest you shall be saved."*

I needed this winter, I reminded myself, in more ways than one. Winter, a resting time for the earth, is a quiet time, a time to wait. And I see, now more than ever, how essential seasons in life are. Each season is a precursor of the next. Without winter, there would be no spring with its new life...no summer in full bloom...no fall with its harvest. Winter is the time when we consider what's gone on before. We think about future plantings, what we may do differently. But for this moment, the fields lie quietly, suspended in silence. The seed dies, is buried, is covered by snow, is pelted by rain. Then we wait for warmth, for sun again. For new growth, for the thaw. For things to move.

As I walked back to my house I thought, *It's going to be wonderful in the mountains next year...waterfalls tumbling, watercress growing in the creek...abundant wildflowers...huckleberry- and gooseberry-laden bushes. But for now, this barren, still winter is beautiful.*

I went into my house, renewed from being in His presence, equipped again to listen and to love because *I* had listened—I had been heard. As Henri Nouwen describes in *The Way of the Heart*, being silent before God protects the inner fire, the life of the Holy Spirit within us. Think about the "seasons" of your life, where you are now. What do you think God is saying to you here?

Prayer
        O Father, thank You for the seasons! You have made us and know how much we need them—times of resting,

of reflection, of work, of planting, and of harvesting. May we embrace fully the season we are in, knowing that it is only for a time, that we may make the most of where we are. We find comfort in Your knowledge of us, knowing that our times are in Your hands. In Jesus' name, amen.

"God does not cease speaking, but the noise of the creature without, and of our passions within, deafens us, and stops our hearing. We must silence every creature, we must silence ourselves, to hear in the deep hush of the whole soul, the ineffable voice of the spouse. We must bend the ear, because it is a gentle and delicate voice..."

—François Fénelon

9

The Great Quest

Behold what manner of love the Father has bestowed on us, that we should be called children of God!

1 JOHN 3:1

I collapsed on the couch that Mother's Day night, over-dosed on cards, flowers, and sentiment. I was still musing over a handmade card I'd received from eight-year-old Chris: *"I'll never forget you,"* he'd written. (Was that good or bad?) And I was pondering the gift of two hamsters from Jon and Eric. I was in no mood to write thank-you notes. With extra company, I'd worked hard in the kitchen and had managed to get the family to church twice that day. My orchid corsage had wilted, and my feet hurt. More than that, I was feeling used. I'd heard of mothers who got breakfast in bed...It sounded messy...But I had worked my fingers to the bone all year. Had anybody noticed?

The cards made me cry. My family thought I was deeply touched, but I'm afraid I was thinking, *So this is it, huh?* I felt like somebody owed me a big-time debt and I was getting a small token payment. As I sat there on the couch and became aware of my feelings, I chided myself: *What do you want? A parade? Neon lights?* I knew I was loved, but why wasn't I *feeling* loved? Why was it that although I worked hard…it somehow was never enough? I dismissed my feelings of exhaustion and unrealistic expectations and went to bed.

Later, I wondered, *Why do I do the things I do, feel the way I feel?* The things that motivate us, the great quests in our lives, are often like chasing rainbows. They are illusions—they evaporate as we move toward them. They change shapes. And yet I persist on my own personal quest—to be loved, to love. A quest shared by many.

We do enormous things to make love happen. We marry the right person, engage ourselves in meaningful work. We try to get our biblical doctrines straight, go to seminars, read books on how to love. In the midst of all this, we are assaulted by *unlove*. The media blitzes us every day with new tales of molestation, abuse, exploitation, violence, perversions of love until we cover our ears with our hands and cry, "Stop! I can't take any more of this ugliness, this opposite of love." And then we see— as I did at the end of a love-designed day—the *unlove* in our own selves.

I'm finding that love cannot be forced. It is like the blossoming of a beautiful rose. God plants the seed of love, then encourages us: "Learn of Me…" And it is in the learning that it happens. When I am all caught up in the doing, that is when I expect results. Payment due for service rendered: *"You owe me…"* It seems that real love is a by-product of something else. "There is no fear in love; but perfect love casts out fear" (1 John 4:18). Jesus says, *You can love because I first loved you.* To experience that love is a lifetime quest.

Jesus whispers, *"You are worth everything to me. I died for you."* And yet I hold Him at arm's length, skeptical. So I accept teaspoonfuls of His love, and then can only give teaspoonfuls of it away.

Why am I afraid to be loved so extravagantly? Is it so hard to believe I don't have to pay? Early imprintations are powerful...In my childhood, we sang of grace but lived works—after all, "the night was coming," and there never is a finish line to work—especially in the spiritual realm. There's always more to do—wrongs to right, and ways to be better, work harder, pray more, be kinder. Loving within the framework of the law—with accounts due and payable—is demanding, relentless. The way to accept His love is realizing *the debt is paid.* I find myself arguing with this—"I must learn to accept Christ's love so I can love in return." But as I read through His Word, He says to me, "No. That is not the way of love. You do not accept this love to do more. *Only accept this love. Abiding in the vine...you bear fruit."*

It seems that when love enters the soul there is an effect. Psalm 23 says, "He restores my soul." To allow Jesus to love me, to restore my soul, I accept His lovingkindness. Hosea 11:4 says, "I drew them with gentle cords, with bands of love. And I was to them as those who take the yoke from their neck."

What does love look like? It is difficult to describe. I saw it in myself the other day when I took the hand of a sick friend and prayed for her. I see it in empathy and understanding for my son. I see it in being able to tell a hard truth covered with mercy. I see it in a gentle touch from my husband, or a simple prayer from my daughter. I see it in newfound respect for myself, a person with limits and failings, a person who needs my own consideration and protection at times. What an amazing and refreshing concept to savor His love, His delight for me. And maybe the result of learning this is that my son Chris will "never forget" that his mother loved him—pure and simple!

If you're struggling with this concept of internalizing God's love for you, take some time to meditate upon it by reading 1 John, as well as 1 Corinthians. *Believe that He loves you.* Over a set period of time (one month is good) keep a little notebook of what you are learning about love. Pray for insights to impact you and your closest relationships.

Prayer

Lord, remind us of what it means to come to You as a little child...to accept Your delight and love for us, just for who we are. May we learn to dwell in Your presence, whether we feel You there or not, and trust what Your Word tells us about Your care for Your people. May we find comfort in knowing that You shelter us in the cleft of the rock and cover us with Your mighty hand. In Jesus' name, amen.

"The Call asks, do you really accept the message that God is head over heels in love with you? I believe that this question is at the core of our ability to mature and grow spiritually. If in our hearts we really don't believe that God loves us as we are, if we are still tainted by the lie that we can do something to make God love us more, we are rejecting the message of the cross."

—Brennan Manning, *The Ragamuffin Gospel*

10

My Place in the Harvest

When He saw the multitudes, He was moved with compassion for them, because they were weary and scattered, like sheep having no shepherd. Then he said to His disciples, "The harvest truly is plentiful, but the laborers are few. Therefore pray the Lord of the harvest to send out laborers into His harvest."

MATTHEW 9:36-38

Mother and Dad were in the dining room discussing the upcoming harvest over coffee. Dad needed to hire extra men; Mother wondered if she should hire a local girl to help with chores. I—a skinny, blonde, ten-year-old girl with big ideas—hung around them, absorbing their excitement, longing to be involved. Harvest was everything, the apex of the year, and there was plenty of work to go around. I interrupted: "I can help out in the field. I can drive the truck! I can cook." Dad looked at me with amusement. "*You?* You can't do anything, you're just a little girl."

Mother, seeing my disappointment, defended me. "She's part of it, Gunder. She can help." And I did find my place in the harvest—in the kitchen, next to Mother.

During harvest, the men would come in at noon for Mother's dinners. Sometimes it was chicken-fried steak, mashed potatoes and gravy, steaming bowls of vegetables, salad, and Mother's famous huckleberry pie for dessert. Always there was plenty...with lots of dishes to wash. In the early evening, Mother would send my sisters and me with a cold supper out to where the men were in the field, so they could work late into the night. We would drive carefully over the bumpy, harvested fields, finding the men by the big red combines that made long shadows against the yellow fields in the late afternoon. Dad and the men were always glad to see us, grateful for the cold drinks we brought in big jugs.

While some of the workers ate, I would watch as the combine poured out the golden grain into the bed of the truck to be hauled to the elevator. I loved every part of it, and I was so glad that my dad allowed me to have a place in the harvest activities.

When I was a teenager, I dreamed of having a place in the Lord's harvest activities, too. At missionary services in our local church, I would sing with the congregation, "I'll go where you want me to go, dear Lord; or mountain, or plain, or sea. I'll say what you want me to say, dear Lord..." Years later, when I was a young mother, I stood with Bill at his ordination service. Shivers went down my spine as we heard the awesome commission: *Preach the Word!* I accepted the challenge along with Bill, finding my place in the harvest field.

Now, at this season of my life, everything seems to change at a dizzying rate. My life today seems dominated by calendars and commitments, and service to Christ becomes complicated by contracts, budgets, and job descriptions. Once again I pray, "Lord, where is my place in Your harvest field?"

Yesterday, Amy and I left the supermarket after shopping for groceries, hurrying so we could get to church on time. The early evening traffic was heavy as we waited to enter the highway. "Mom," Amy said, softly. "Look." A young woman stood next to our car, holding a sign: *Hungry. Will work for food.* Amy said, "Mom, I can give her the box of animal crackers that I just bought." We watched as the woman faced the heavy stream of traffic, an unreadable expression on her young face, maybe of desperate bravado. I opened my mouth to tell Amy that this was probably a racket, that she most likely earned lots of money off people's guilt as they exited the grocery store. Instead I said lamely, "I guess we could share some of our groceries." We circled back into the parking lot and fixed up a bag of groceries, with Amy's box of animal crackers on top. We drove back to the woman, and as Amy handed her the bag, the woman began to cry. "God bless you," she said. Moved, Amy and I left in tears, too. What a simple, small thing—to give a hungry person food. Yet it somehow felt pivotal, profound.

As we drove, I thought about the deeper hunger people have—the hunger for the Bread of Life, Jesus. I was quick to assume that afternoon that the woman's "God bless you" indicated she knew about Jesus, but maybe that wasn't the case. Sometimes I regret we didn't take more time to make sure she had spiritual food as well as a bag of groceries.

I'm seeing that the biggest step to being involved in the harvest is simply to be aware that there *is* one. My life can be so scheduled with Christian activities that I can forget the *lost*. The lost are all around us—our neighbors, our friends, our family members—and Jesus always shines the brightest from us when we allow people directly into our lives despite our flaws and simply give out of what He has given us.

It doesn't really matter what job we have in the harvest. What matters is whether or not we are willing to be involved. The Lord of the harvest says, "You are needed in the kingdom. The harvest is great, and the laborers are few."

What is your place in the harvest? Are you willing to see the lost? Are you willing to be His hand extended? Are you willing to allow the Lord to use you?

Remember that God always deals with us where we are, with what we have. It can be intimidating to witness about Jesus, but when we are fully in love with Him ourselves, it is natural to share Him with others. Remember that it's relationship, not religion, that people need. We only must be willing to share out of what He has given us.

What a great joy to be able to give the Bread of heaven to a world that so desperately needs Him. Spiritual harvests are preceded by prayer and the sowing of the Word of God. If you are wondering how you can be involved in a more vital way in God's harvest field, begin now to pray, to seek God earnestly. Then wait for Him to show you your place—He will often use you just where you are.

Prayer

Lord, I do not say, "Be with me," for of course, You *are!* I say, "May my eyes be open to Your Presence." May my spirit be open to You in a fresh way, and may I so burn with Your contagious love for the lost that others are drawn to You. Help me to see the harvest—wherever I am—and joyfully accept my place in it. In Jesus' name, amen.

"Understanding what God is about to do where you are is more important than telling God what you want to do for Him...God hasn't told us to go away and do some work for Him. He has told us that He is already at work trying to bring a lost world to Himself. If we will adjust our lives to Him in a love relationship, He will show us where He is at work."

—Henry Blackaby, *Experiencing God*

11

Mountain Climbing

*We can rejoice, too, when we run into problems and
trials, for we know that they are good for us—they
help us learn to endure. And endurance develops
strength of character in us, and character strength-
ens our confident expectation of salvation. And this
expectation will not disappoint us. For we know
how dearly God loves us, because he has given us
the Holy Spirit to fill our hearts with his love.*

ROMANS 5:3-5 NLT

It was not easy to get there, but the memory of it draws
me. I long to revisit that beautiful meadow lying near
the summit of a rugged mountain not far from my home.

Friends told Bill and me that the hike was worth the
effort, so several summers ago, with three of our children—Chris, Andy, and Amy—we started out. As we
marched up single file through a tunnel of trees, the path
seemed to go nowhere. It wound up and around for miles
through tall stands of trees. Several times we found ourselves at a fork in the path, and we wondered which of
the paths that angled out was the main one. As we
trudged upward, we were not always sure that we had
stayed on the right course. The path itself was rocky,
tedious, and dangerous.

When the kids grumbled about their aching legs or
when one of us nearly twisted an ankle, I began to

wonder if the difficulty was worth it. But then—just when I thought the trip had been a ridiculous waste of a summer Saturday—the fragrance of wildflowers filled the air. *How could this be?* I thought. *It's dark here. The sunlight is blocked by dense trees.* The floor of the forest was quiet and barren beneath the moss hanging from tall firs. But soon the path widened, and there it was: a beautiful, sun-drenched meadow fed by streams that cascaded from a glacier clinging to the side of the mountain. We caught our breath. It was too lovely to imagine.

The meadow was a mass of wildflowers of every variety, growing so thickly that the meadow reminded me of an enormous English garden. Enchanted, we took off our shoes and sat by the stream. *Surely this must be like heaven,* we thought. We ate our lunch, savoring our surroundings. All too soon it was time to go back.

As we made our way down the mountain, I thought of Jesus and His disciples up on the Mount of Transfiguration, when God's glory came and Moses and Elijah spoke with Jesus (see Luke 9:28-36). I can identify with Peter, who, during this glorious mountaintop experience with the Lord, suggested, "Let's build a temple here so that we can come here often and make this last forever!"

Like Peter, I would like to enshrine the mountaintop experiences, to capture those rare places of victory when I sense God's presence, His pleasure in me. Certain times in my life are like the sun-drenched meadow. I love the times when I feel at one with my husband and we hold each other, awed at being in love nearly 30 years. Being a mother is wonderful when things are going well with

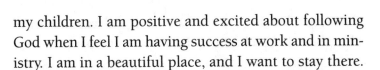

my children. I am positive and excited about following God when I feel I am having success at work and in ministry. I am in a beautiful place, and I want to stay there.

But to be honest, those times are rare. Many more times of my life are like the climbing up the mountain—exhausting, uncertain, painful, tedious. Bill and I have had rocky times. Sometimes mothering is very hard work. Some days the ministry God has called me to feels as if it isn't going anywhere.

But the longer I live, the more convinced I am that the struggle—the journey itself—is significant, necessary. For the "joy that was set before Him," Jesus endured the cross (Hebrews 12:2). Endurance is a difficult path, and often it's lonely. And yet struggle is honest and very, very human.

During a long illness, a friend of mine asked, "Has my life made a difference? Has all of this been worth it?" She, like most of us, wanted her life to count. When the Lord revealed to her that He was using her life—and her struggle—to encourage others, she found the courage to endure the long journey of illness, which recently ended in her death. She persisted because she trusted that the journey had purpose.

Perhaps there is something in your life now that is a struggle for you—even though you know it is right—and you are tempted to give up. Many voices today would tell you that nobody should have to work this hard, that nothing is worth this kind of pain. But the battle is won not so much in blinding moments of truth as it is in hanging in there when the going is tough. Don't give up.

If you are following the Lord, the path will lead to a beautiful place. Keep climbing. It is worth the pain.

Remember that there are songs yet to be sung. Paintings yet to be created. Books yet to be written. Lives to be touched for God. Families to be forged. Marriages to be crafted. Lives of integrity yet to be lived. For you to attain these things, you must persevere, stay on the path, and allow God's Word to light your way (see Psalm 119:105).

On our hike, when the path seemed darkest we caught the fragrance of wildflowers. I believe that if we open our awareness to God in the midst of our struggles, we will find that the fragrance of His presence is with us. And His presence will urge us to stay the course. "Do not throw away this confident trust in the Lord, no matter what happens. Remember the great reward it brings you! Patient endurance is what you need now, so you will continue to do God's will. Then you will receive all that he has promised" (Hebrews 10:35-36 NLT).

Prayer

Lord, sometimes we get a vision of a lovely ideal You call us to—something we can do or be. Then we begin the journey, and we find it is hard. Sometimes it feels too hard and lonely, and we're tempted to give up. Lord, keep before us Your example—to purchase our redemption, You endured the cross for us. We humbly thank You and rejoice that in our human struggles, You are perfecting us and helping us become real followers of You. In Christ's name, amen.

"If we are going to live as disciples of Jesus, we have to remember that all noble things are difficult. The Christian life is gloriously difficult, but the difficulty of it does not make us faint and cave in, it rouses us up to overcome."

—Oswald Chambers, *My Utmost for His Highest*

12

Leaving Home, Going Home

Lord, You have been our dwelling place in all generations. Before the mountains were brought forth, or ever You had formed the earth and the world, even from everlasting to everlasting, you are God...Let Your work appear to Your servants, and Your glory to their children. And let the beauty of the LORD our God be upon us, and establish the work of our hands for us; yes, establish the work of our hands.

PSALM 90:1-2,16-17

I kiss my daughter, who is still snuggled in her bed, her hair a dark tousled mass. I look in on Andy, who is sleeping the wholehearted sleep of a growing teenager, and walk downstairs, feeling a twinge of guilt. Two of our older sons are just now leaving for work, and I stretch tall to hug them goodbye.

Bill drives me to the airport in the early dawn, and as we travel, we share a fragrant cup of coffee and talk. We have anxieties about parenting growing-up children. We haven't done this before, and it's scary. How do we let go? Yes, this feels like a bad time to leave the family (I've been gone too much), but this weekend is a reunion of the little country school I attended for eight years, and I don't want to miss it. And besides, I'm really wanting to go back home to the farm. It's been a long time.

In the airport I watch people—families separating, reuniting. I watch a woman cry as she says goodbye to a man. A group of college boys—their faces fresh, optimistic—hurry by with backpacks slung over their shoulders. A young couple with two small children carry diaper bags, stroller, and toys. I remember, when our children were small, older women would whisper to me, as if to share a secret, "These are the best times..." I would usually smile and nod, but as I scrambled to care for little wiggly bodies would often think with consternation, "This is *it?*" I remember being consumed by our children's needs when they were small, when my world felt so defined. I feel a sudden pang for those days. How is it that we can be so involved...and then just disappear, like dandelion seeds blowing in the wind?

My mother and sister arrive on their connecting flight to go with me to the reunion, and I guide my aging mother through the security gate as I would a small child—encouraging, coaxing. She can't understand the wait and wants to go home. "When are we there?" "Soon, Mother." "I want to go home." *Home? Where is home?* "You *are* going home, Mother. To the farm in Montana, to see the boys and their families."

My brother Dan is at the airport to meet us at this ruggedly magnificent place that nurtured us. I eagerly drink in the view—the rolling plains, the majestic Rockies off to the west. The farm where I grew up is now Dan's place, and he and his wife Nancy have tended it well. The lawns are green, the garden is up, the barn has a new coat of paint. The crops haven't had enough rain, but they're being irrigated, and they look good. Dan always loved home.

Early the next morning, I walk down the familiar graveled road past the farmhouse. The air is full of the meadowlark's song as I walk over to where the little country school used to be. It was moved off its foundation and is now a Baptist church in a neighboring town. All that remains is an open basement. I can still see a shuffleboard triangle painted on the concrete. This impossibly small place that had once been a big part of my world is deserted, overgrown with weeds. Memories flood me. In this place, we memorized Tennyson, Sandburg, Whitman. Here, we formed a strong sense of community.

The reunion was marked by laughter, reminiscences, and amazement that all we children were now middle-aged. As the time came for me to leave, I was homesick, missing Bill, missing the children. Missing home. Would someday grown-up children make pilgrimages back to our home, and would they remember good times? As I flew back to Oregon, I thought of my childhood dream—to have a Home—a place of learning about God, a place of laughter, of music. A safe place. For years now when I come home from my walks I stand back in the trees and pray, *Bless this house, Lord. Bless Bill, Jon, Eric, Chris, Andy, Amy. All who come here.*

Lately, though, I feel I've been praying for a depot instead of a home. Suitcases, duffel bags are always in the entry as people come and go. My people, my children, leaving home. It's natural...it's time...but there is pain in the tearing away. And I struggle not so much with new places as I do with the transitions—the breath-holding, connecting flights that take me—where? And I often beg, "Put me back, Lord, in that familiar place. How it used to be." But this place of transition is showing me that this "house for God" that I have so wanted to craft…is *me*.

What an incredible thought—*We are His dwelling place in the world!* And, "unless the Lord builds the house, they that build it labor in vain." Everything else changes around us. But the relationship we have with Him lasts for eternity. As we yield our lives to Him, He will gently shape us, clean us, and make us a place where love reigns. In the swirling winds of change, we have the privilege to make *Him* our security, our wholeness. Our home.

Prayer

Thank You, Father, for the metaphors You place so strongly in our lives. What we all long for is Home—a place of security and peace, and loving acceptance. The homes we establish on this earth are transient and changing, as wonderful as they are. But they are only a poor reflection of the amazing home You offer us—Your very eternal Presence in our lives! You also offer us a home made in the heavens, not made with hands. Come into our hearts, Lord Jesus. We welcome You and rejoice in knowing You as our eternal home. In Christ's name, amen.

"The soul's house, that interior dwelling place which we all possess, for the upkeep of which we are responsible— is a place in which we can meet God, or from which in a sense we can exclude God."

—Evelyn Underhill, *The House of the Soul*

13

The Door of Prayer

Rejoice always, pray without ceasing, in everything give thanks; for this is the will of God in Christ Jesus for you...With thanksgiving, let your requests be made known to God; and the peace of God which surpasses all understanding, will guard your hearts and minds through Christ Jesus.

1 THESSALONIANS 5:16-18; PHILIPPIANS 4:6-7

When I was a girl, on Saturdays I would stay in town with my grandmother so I could have my piano lesson. The walk to my teacher's house took me by a convent, and I would slow my steps, secretly intrigued by the sisters praying in the chapel. My Grandma Olson, a practical, no-nonsense woman who'd raised four children alone in the Depression, was not impressed. "You can't be so heavenly-minded you're no earthly good," she would say. I thought wistfully that if a person wanted to be a person of prayer she had to be sort of holy...mystical. Certainly not wear blue jeans and ride bikes and laugh a lot, which I liked to do (and still do). But even then, my heart yearned after Him, aware of the God-shaped vacuum that only He could fill, the thirst that could be quenched by the Living Water only He could give.

When I was a child, I prayed to accept Jesus as my Savior. After that, now and then I would shoot up quick prayers, especially when I was in trouble. I received a jolt one morning when, as a freshman in college, I came to class ill-prepared for the test the professor was handing out. Then he had the nerve to pray, "Lord, bring to remembrance what each student has studied." I needed him to pray for a miracle for me to know the answers! It began to occur to me that God is more than a genie in a bottle.

It was when I was a young mother with a toddler and a new baby that I tentatively tried the door of prayer. Bill had taken a new job as a youth pastor, and I felt very alone, in over my head with parenting and church responsibilities. One Sunday evening in church as I sat in the back cradling my little ones, I offered up this simple prayer: "*yes.*" All I could do, I told God, was offer myself to Him just as I was. Over the years I've prayed this prayer many times. Sometimes the prayer sticks in my throat. Sometimes I pray it with fresh urgency. But with that step I began to understand: *Prayer is being available to God.* An astounding concept, to think He calls me His beloved, and I dare to call Him my Friend. To know that this relationship can deepen through the years as He calls for me to open the door of my heart ever wider to Him.

I think so often of Jesus' two friends, Mary and Martha. Mary was the one who sat at His feet, while Martha rushed about serving (see Luke 10). I tend to identify with Martha—the "Grandma Olson" in me tells me I should *do* something, and I find it hard to *wait*...After all, I rationalize, prayer can be as practical as asking for daily bread, even though Jesus clearly said that Mary was the one who had her priorities straight.

In 2 Kings 4:8-37, there is a story of another woman who learned to wait on God. The "Shunammite woman" was well known for her hospitality and philanthropy, and she even added a wing to her home for the use of the prophet Elisha. In gratitude, Elisha asked her what she needed. "Nothing," she said (not being given to whining, as I am). And yet she did have a need—she was barren. In time, God gave her and her husband a son, and as the Scripture says, the boy grew. But one tragic day that boy, who'd been out in the field with his father, came in complaining of a headache—and soon he died in his mother's arms. The Shunammite woman's reaction was amazing: She placed the lifeless body of her son on Elisha's bed, closed the door, and went to find Elisha, telling her husband everything was all right. When Elisha saw her coming in the distance, he knew something was terribly wrong, yet her first greeting was, "It is well." Elisha went back with her to the room where the boy lay and shut himself in, and God miraculously restored life to the boy.

As Bill and I drove home yesterday from speaking at a family conference, I thought of the devastated young father we had spoken to, whose wife was leaving him and their two small children. His story was not unique among many others we had heard—and on the drive home, I felt as if I'd waded through the casualties on a major Civil War battlefield, dispensing Band-Aids and aspirin when situations called for intensive care. When confronted by such chaos and pain, easy answers are stripped from me, and I feel struck dumb. How could I have told that young man, "Just pray and trust God. All will be well"?

Scripture says to "Pray without ceasing." Often I am aware of His Presence, but some days His absence is all that I feel. I'm learning, though, that it's all right to feel helpless and desperate before God. Andrew Murray wrote, "Never forget the two foundational-truths on which this blessed waiting rests:...thy absolute helplessness; the absolute sufficiency of thy God." Desperation is what drives me into His presence, and like the Shunammite woman, I can "shut the door" on my burden—lifeless and broken as it is—and leave it with Him, knowing that He is the Redeemer, the One who makes everything beautiful in its time.

I don't live a cloistered life, and yet...*I do*...because when I enter the door of prayer and worship Him in the innermost chamber of my heart, I see *Him*, mighty to save. The circumstances that so consume my prayers become God's business, not mine. I say with David, "My eyes are ever on the LORD" (Psalm 25:15 NIV).

Find a quiet place with your Bible and prayerfully consider these questions: Is my relationship with God deepening or growing colder? Where do I feel I can grow? Am I willing to hear His still, small voice and be obedient to His Word? Am I praying with "worship" or with "worry"?

Prayer

    Lord...You know our hearts and deepest conflicts. We long to be used wholly for You, but sometimes life trips us up, and we get ambushed by our own humanity…by others' humanity. But "whom have I on earth beside Thee?" Father God, remind us that our lives are broken without Your touch. You can be bigger to us than our failures and weaknesses. Remind us that You long for us too, so that You may touch us and heal us. Our eyes are ever on You, Lord, and in this we take refuge. In Jesus' name, amen.

"We all come to prayer with a tangled mass of motives—altruistic and selfish, merciful and hateful, loving and bitter. Frankly, this side of eternity we will never unravel the good from the bad, the pure from the impure. But what I have come to see is that God is big enough to receive us with all our mixture. We do not have to be bright, or pure, or filled with faith, or anything. That is what grace means, and not only are we saved by grace, we live by it as well. And we pray by it."

—Richard Foster, *Prayer: Finding the Heart's True Home*

"O Lord my God, Light of the blind, and Strength of the weak; yea also Light of those that see, and strength of the strong: hearken unto my soul, and hear it crying out of the depths."

—Augustine

14

Encouragement: A Gift from the Heart

*Anxiety in the heart of man causes depression,
but a good word makes it glad.*

PROVERBS 12:25

It was Monday morning, and I sat on the couch in my robe, feeling swamped. Not so much by the big challenges as by the "chronic-ness" of life. Phone calls I needed to make. Bills. The dirty house. Writing deadlines. Projects that needed attention. Family relationships that seemed to circle around the same arguments, the same difficulties. *Laundry*...I stared at the huge pile of socks before me. Laundry seemed representative of my life somehow. As I sorted socks, I thought, *It's always the same old "stuff" that needs tending.*

All of us have some of that "same old stuff"—chronic, routine things that need ongoing attention. And we need help at times just to keep going, to face another day. Sometimes we need an extra boost from someone who will say, "Keep going—you can make it!" In a word, we need encouragement.

Seventeen years ago, Bill was speaking at a convention on parenting while I was trying to manage our three unruly little sons in the back of the auditorium. We were all tired, and I was on the verge of tears, wishing I was home. At that moment, an elderly pastor sat down near me. "You remind me of my wife when we were young," he said. "She always had to take care of the kids in church alone. But you know what?" He leaned closer, his eyes bright. "We raised eight of the greatest kids. We love them so much! Don't worry about having to do everything right. Just love them—they'll be fine." He got up and left, never knowing his words were *life* to me.

Four years ago, struggling with chronic pain, I was in the doctor's office again, crying, "I am so tired of pain! How do I go on?" My doctor said kindly, "I *do* see progress. You're just in a little dip right now. Don't be discouraged—keep on." I doggedly stuck to the exercise regime, the therapy—and sure enough, now I am enjoying health. His words inspired me to keep on.

There have been times when I've sat down to write and I've prayed, *"Lord, show me what to write. I have nothing to give."* An idea comes, and then a note from a reader that says, "This was just what I needed to hear." These letters remind me of Proverbs 25:25: "As cold water to a weary soul, so is good news from a far country."

When we encourage others in their neediest moments (and sometimes we are unaware of just how deep the need is), we offer them a lifeline, something to hold on to when the waves of life threaten to pull them under.

Proverbs 18:21 says, "Death and life are in the power of the tongue, and those who love it will eat its fruit." Think of it: You can literally offer someone *life* by an encouraging word, a smile, or taking a moment to try to understand what he or she is going through. A phone call and a sincere "How are you—really?" can be so simple, yet so important.

Think of a time when someone encouraged you. Do you remember the impact it had? What did that person do? Did she write a note, make a phone call, offer a listening ear over a cup of coffee or tea, clean your bathroom, watch your kids? No doubt someone in your life needs encouragement right now. It may be a co-worker, a member of your own family, or someone else you see on a daily basis. Try to imagine the unique pressures he or she is facing, and prayerfully look for opportunities to offer encouragement.

Prayer

Lord, thank You for those times when Your Spirit has spoken words of comfort, wisdom, and encouragement to our hearts through one of Your people. Teach us to look beyond our own chronic, ordinary problems to see the needs of others. Remind us, Lord, that "death and life are in the power of the tongue." May our words be life to those in need of encouragement. In Christ's name, amen.

"If I am inconsiderate about the comfort of others, or their feelings, or even their little weaknesses; if I am careless about their little hurts and miss opportunities to smooth their way...then I know nothing of Calvary love."

—Amy Carmichael, *If*

15

Faith of My Father

Sow for yourselves righteousness; reap in mercy;
break up your fallow ground, for it is time to seek
the LORD, till He comes and rains righteousness on
you.

HOSEA 10:12

I close my eyes and remember what it was like to be 12 in the month of May. Sunlight streamed into the one-room schoolhouse as I tried to keep my mind on my book. Through the open window I heard a yellow-breasted meadowlark, as well as the faraway drone of my father's tractor as he plowed, getting the ground ready for seed. The winter had been long—harsh at times, as storms had swept across the rolling wheat fields of northern Montana. But in May, the Rocky Mountains off to the west somehow looked closer and gentler, and the glaciers glistened with fresh snow. The trees around our house began to leaf out, and dandelions brought cheery splashes of yellow.

On Saturdays in May, Dad would enlist my brother, my sister, and me to go with him into the field to pull out the biggest rocks so they wouldn't choke the wheat he would soon plant. As I bounced along on the bed of the pickup, I wondered at the big rocks that kept turning up from somewhere deep in the earth. *Every year there were more…Where did they come from?*

Spring plowing ("summer fallowing," we called it) was dirty business. Dad would come in from the field covered with dirt, but happy. He seemed to have a special feeling about spring—the breaking up of the hard ground, the preparation of the soil to receive the seed. Spring meant promise, hope. Forget last year's drought—forget the hail that wiped out the winter wheat—here was another spring, a new chance at harvest.

Today, newly warm air and songbirds remind me of home and springtime. I find myself pausing to sit in the sun, remembering the warm smell of freshly turned earth. I must leave soon to go with my husband to speak at a family conference, and I sit in my favorite place—a bench outside my front door—cherishing home, reluctant to leave. My daughter, Amy, and I have exchanged gifts until we're together again: She has lent me her teddy bear angel; I have lent her Mother's small Bible to keep next to her bed until I get home. Just before I gave it to her, I read what Dad had written to her on the flyleaf: *"To my beloved wife, Harriet. You are the light of the world. A city that is set on a hill cannot be hid."* His angular script, written with a blue fountain pen, leaps out at me—and it seems as if his words are meant for me, too.

Dad was a man of few words. He found it difficult to talk about his deep love of God, family, and the land. But he lived out his faith for us. Every morning before my siblings and I left for school, he would read the King James Version of the Bible to us. He liked the Psalms: *"I will lift up mine eyes unto the hills, from whence cometh my help. My help cometh from the LORD, which made heaven and earth"* (Psalm 121:1-2 KJV). My dad felt closest to God when he was out in the field, looking toward the mountains. When we moved to Oregon, he felt hemmed in by all the trees because, as he said, he "liked to see."

My father's life provided a rich soil for my faith to grow, and I am grateful. Yes, his life had "rocks"—those fallen, human parts that kept coming to the surface. In his own way he tried to remove the obstacles that prevented growth in his life. He suffered great losses, but he bore them with grace and dignity. For him, the best solutions for sorrow were to help someone else and to saturate his brokenness in God's Word.

We are our own soil—there is no doubt about that. You and I also have troublesome rocks that seem to come to the surface of our lives and prevent growth. The rocks may be our anxieties, our difficult relationships, our selfishness, or any number of other obstacles. Like the farmer, we need to be willing to pull out the rocks and break up the fallow ground. For me, that sometimes means disturbing my life, turning over my assumptions about how God works, plowing up my assumptions about my place in His field. I need to come once again to a place of receptivity where the Word of God can take root in my life and grow. I need to be tender, fresh, giving God a place to express His will for me. Like spring plowing, this process can be messy. Sometimes it is very hard, but without it, I will not be a place where God's seed can grow.

Becoming a receptive place for seed to grow isn't a one-time thing—it must be done seasonally for continued harvests. For instance, at this season of my life, it is difficult for me to leave home. I would rather stay where it is comfortable. But I choose to see that God is breaking up the ground in my life to make me more fruitful. Just as my dad willingly participated in the seasons, doing what the occasion required, I need to remember that life, too, has its seasons. If I want God to be able to reap a harvest through my life, I need to be willing to let Him prepare the soil—even if that means experiencing discomfort or pain or humbling experiences of waiting.

What about you? Do you sense that you have rocks that need to be removed before you will be more receptive to spiritual growth? Have you asked God to do spring plowing in your life? Have you invited Him to break up the hard places? I encourage you to allow Him to do it, even if it feels painful. Take some time to study the "seed and soil" passage from Matthew 13, and think about how God is preparing you to be more receptive so His Word and His will can take root.

Prayer

Lord, how often we say that we want You to use us, that we want to be all we can be for You. And yet we realize that means You will break up the fallow ground in our lives. That process may be painful. But we invite

You to do it because we want to be receptive soil in which Your Word and Your will can grow. Give us courage and willingness to be disturbed and corrected and softened. May we gladly stay in Your program, knowing that You are working all things for our good. Lord, we yield our all to You. In Jesus' name, amen.

"I have been reflecting on the inestimable value of 'broken things.' Broken pitchers gave ample light for victory (Judges 7:19-21); broken bread was more than enough for all the hungry (Matthew 14:19-21); broken box gave fragrance to all the world (Mark 14:3,9); and broken body is salvation to all who believe and receive the Savior (Isaiah 53:5-6,12; 1 Corinthians 11:24). And what cannot the Broken One do with our broken plans, projects, and heart?"

—V. Raymond Edman

"Sow the Word of God, and everyone who listens will get to God. If you sow vows, resolutions, aspirations, emotions, you will reap nothing but exhaustion…'and you shall sow your seed in vain, for your enemies shall eat it'; but sow the Word of God, and as sure as God is God, it will bring forth fruit."

—Oswald Chambers, from *Oswald Chambers: The Best from All His Books*

"Heart troubles in God's husbandry are not wounds, but the putting in of the spade before planting the seeds."

—Henry Ward Beecher

Final Prayer

Take, Lord, and receive all my liberty, my memory, my understanding and my entire will—all that I have and call my own. You have given it all to me. To You, Lord, I return it. Everything is Yours; do with it what You will. Give me only Your love and Your grace. That is enough for me.

—Ignatius of Loyola

16

The Window of Hope

*[As] it is impossible for God to lie, we might have
strong consolation, who have fled for refuge to lay
hold of the hope set before us. This hope we have
as an anchor of the soul, both sure and steadfast.*

HEBREWS 6:18-19

Deadlines and a speaking engagement were staring me
in the face, but that didn't stop family life. The phone
was ringing, Chris was packing for his move to Portland, Amy and a friend were roaming throughout the
house. Bill was doing office work, and I secretly envied
his ability to shut out all distractions and focus on the
task at hand. My home office often feels like the middle
of the freeway. I knew I had to find a quiet place. But
where? It was stormy outside, and there seemed no place
to go.

And then I had an inspiration: Andy's room! At the
very top of our house on the third level is a small bed-
room with a sloped ceiling that we call the "boys' room."
First it was Jon and Eric's room; then it was Chris's; now
it's Andy's, and he is away at college. It was perfect—
too far away to hear the phone and people downstairs.

I lugged up a few things to add some ambiance to the basketball poster–dominated room: my portable CD player and a mug of tea. I'd been up in this room many times to pick up laundry, or to clean, to pray with the guys, to give them a hug or a "mom lecture." And always when I had come to this room before, I had only seen them—they and their needs had filled my vision. Now, in their absence, this was a different place.

The row of shelves above Andy's desk spoke of previous occupants: school annuals…boxes of treasured baseball cards…a collection of hats…trophies…pictures of friends and family. There were a couple of little stuffed animals that mutely waited for boys who'd abandoned them long ago. I tried hard not to see the dust or feel the yearning and nostalgia inside me.

The single large window framed a view of the massive pine tree outside the house, offering a filtered glimpse beyond of sky and distant mountains. It was beautiful, peaceful. As I sipped my tea, I thought, *How odd…In this house where I've lived for 17 years I am unexpectedly in a new place.* Seeing Andy's room with new eyes was a great reminder that it isn't the circumstances as much as how I perceive the circumstances. When I look at a frustrating or seemingly dead-end situation through the new lens of hope and possibility, I am in an entirely new place. We can choose to see hope and new possibilities.

Looking out Andy's window, I thought of the Bible story in 1 Samuel 19 and 2 Samuel 6. I was intrigued by the imagery: First, Michal helps David, whom she loved, out a window to escape Saul's wrath; later, she watches

David through a window as he triumphantly leads the return of the ark of the covenant.

But how much the framing, the perspective, changed Michal's view. The second time, she saw David with disgust, revulsion. It's true Michal had been treated badly by the men in her life. She had a right to feel betrayed, but her anger turned to bitterness—and Scripture says the lens through which Michal saw her circumstances brought barrenness to her life, a wilderness of lost hope.

Michal was closed in, trapped by her circumstances. However, I'm learning that when I look at a frustrating or negative situation through the window of hope and possibility, I am in an entirely new place. I'm reminded of this truth by finding an unexpected haven in Andy's room!

Another word for hope is "expectation." The Three Sisters mountains that tower over us—named by the early settlers "Faith, Hope, and Charity"—are magnificent mountains; but it's *Hope,* the middle mountain, that captivates me these days. "Hope" is the mountain pass—the way *through*…the expectation that God will provide an answer even though we can't see one right away.

Do you have a seemingly "negative situation" in your life, a place where perhaps you feel stuck or frustrated? Step back mentally from the situation and consider how you can reframe it through the eyes of hope, see the new possibilities in the same old circumstances. Read through Romans 5:1-11 and 8:24-25 and think about this: God's plan for you is peace, a good future, and hope. As you comprehend God's intentions toward you, how does this help you build up hope?

We can identify with David, who said, "Why are you cast down, O my soul? And why are you disquieted within me? Hope in God; for I shall yet praise Him" (Psalm 43:5). *Hope reminds us of realities we can't yet see...*the reality that, because we are His, God is at work in our lives no matter how it seems, and we can move ahead with hope, with expectation.

Prayer

Lord, there is so much You want to do through us if we will only look at our circumstances with eyes of faith. Thank You for the unique and varied situations You give to each one of us. We pray we will be faithful stewards of them and look to You as our source. Help us to exercise the necessary discipline to think on the things that are "pure, and lovely and of good report." May we set our hope upon You, always. In Jesus' name, amen.

"Christianity declares that we are 'saved by hope.' It also declares that we are 'saved by faith.' There is no contradiction. Hope and faith are twin sisters. They always cooperate...Christianity declares that God is a 'God of hope.' Our confidence in ourselves lags a long way behind God's confidence in us. He expects much more from man than man can yet imagine. The apostle says that a man 'without hope' is a man 'without God,' and urges us 'to abound in hope'...Despair is demoralizing; hope is inspiring. Doubt is debilitating; hope is energizing."

—W.T. McElveen

17

Root of Bitterness

Looking carefully lest anyone fall short of the grace of God; lest any root of bitterness springing up cause trouble, and by this many become defiled.

HEBREWS 12:15

California has its earthquakes, the Midwest its tornadoes, the Southeast coast its hurricanes. In the Northwest we have our forest fires—and after a hot, dry summer, we are especially vulnerable. There's an old charred tree standing near my house, evidence that a fire swept through here once.

Not long ago a volunteer firefighter knocked at our door, telling us what we needed to do in case of fire. I wondered, *If we ever had to evacuate, what would I take?* People first, of course. Spooky, our cat. Our photo albums, slides, the kids' baby books and scrapbooks, my journals, our computers. My list grew. It would be a full pickup load if we had time.

Our local fire department is vigilant, cautious. In the spring, we must rake dried brush and pine needles from around the house. There are to be no fireworks of any kind here in the mountains. Campfires are to be carefully monitored and must be extinguished when leaving a campsite. A few years ago after someone had burned dead brush and tree stumps, a fire began to smolder underground, going through the root system. Our soil, formed of lava thousands of years ago, is so porous and rocky with air pockets in some places that the fire was actually able to burn *underground*. The fire came above ground a few miles away and caused a forest fire in which several homes were destroyed. Friends of ours had their home completely destroyed by this fire that got in the root system, surprising everyone with its consuming intensity when it emerged later.

Roots are an efficient network, feeding the plant, making it grow. Some roots, especially young ones, come out easily when pulled. But then there are those stubborn ones that go deep and strong. They are the ones that have a history, that have been allowed to flourish... that have been nurtured and fed.

Scripture talks about the awesome power of the "root of bitterness" and how it can destroy lives. How does a root of bitterness grow? Perhaps from justice denied, or an expectation unmet. Anger unresolved and smoldering, maybe from an offense at the hands of people we love. How easily it happens, takes root. We think, *He should have known better.* Or, *If he would just say he was sorry.* Or, *She needs to make restitution for this.* Or, *God could have prevented this from happening. And He didn't.*

I can be bitter at myself, too, mentally flogging myself for past mistakes. Or bitter at the unrighteous in our nation, thinking in some twisted way that I'm doing God a favor by being mad at sinners. Maybe it comes from wishing I were in God's place, thinking, *This wouldn't have happened if I were in charge.* Bitterness comes from a belief I deserve better than what I have received. Bitterness is nasty stuff.

And the more life experiences we have, the more opportunities we have for bitterness. The amazing thing is how it can spread through an entire life; how it can suddenly spring up, entwining everything in its path—and we wonder, "Where did *that* come from?"

How does one let go of offenses, of deeply rooted things that slowly but surely sap the life from us? In John chapter 21, Jesus is making breakfast on the seashore for His disciples after they'd forsaken and denied Him. There was something healing, poignant, in the gesture. It was forgiveness, but it was more than that. It was grace and mercy offered—grace and mercy received with humility, out of hunger and need.

We can receive healing from bitterness when we see our own sin and need for forgiveness. This awareness softens the hard ground that surrounds this stubborn root—and even when we can't deal with the root itself, as we let go, *He* deals with it. "Through the Lord's mercies," the prophet wrote in Lamentations 3:22, "we are not consumed."

Our friends whose home was destroyed rebuilt their house on the original foundation. We too can be restored when our foundation is on Him. Jesus said to forgive seventy times seven, if necessary (see Matthew 18:21-35).

It's not a onetime thing: Some stubborn roots need more attention, just as some chronic wounds need more applications of ointment.

Read Hebrews 12:11-17 and Matthew 18:21-35 and take some time to prayerfully ask yourself, *Am I bitter? Am I secretly nursing grudges or wrongs? Do I have one standard for others and another for myself? Have I caused bitterness or resentment in anyone else? What does it take to stand before God with clean hands and a pure heart?*

If you are still struggling with the feeling of bitterness, write out the "wrong" in detail on a piece of paper. Then pray, *"Lord, I give this to You, the perfect judge. I relinquish my hold on this person, this situation. I trust You with the outcome."* Find a time when you can burn the paper in the fireplace or otherwise tangibly destroy it. Then when you are tempted to relive this offense, remember that you have given it to God.

Prayer

Lord, Thank You for Your grace and mercy, which continue to pursue us even when we forget what You've done for us in the past. Forgive us for slipping back into old ways of holding on to things that seem comfortable to us yet are not Your will. Thank You for taking the time to clean out the impurities, even though the process may be painful. Help us to walk in newness of life, Lord, to be aware of Your powerful forgiveness. Shine the truth of Your Word upon us and give us the ability to extend forgiveness to others. In Jesus' name, amen.

"Keeping kills. Relinquishing heals…We do not quickly divest ourselves. But the question will have been put… An invitation will have been issued. Return to the command, to the God who rests and gives rest, who sets free and satisfies…We do not yield easily. But…if we do not yield, we shall die."

—Walter Brueggemann, *Finally Comes the Poet*

18

Crossroad Choices

I set before you today life and prosperity, death and destruction. For I command you today to love the LORD *your God, to walk in his ways, and to keep his commands, decrees and laws...Now choose life, so that you and your children may live and that you may love the* LORD *your God, listen to his voice, and hold fast to him. For the* LORD *is your life.*

DEUTERONOMY 30:15-16,19-20 NIV

It was strange, standing before the student body of the college my husband and I had attended 25 years previously. Two of our sons were now students there, and Eric, our second oldest, dressed in Bermuda shorts, introduced us as speakers for the day.

In the late '60s, boys had sat on one side of the chapel, girls on the other. Certainly no shorts had been allowed. But looking back, I had the oddest sensation that I had something to say to my college-self...a young woman with an unwrinkled face and unlimited dreams. I was in love with life and a young man named Bill Carmichael. Life beckoned. Anything was possible.

If I could, I would say to that young woman, "*Nancie!* You are grabbing the hand of that wonderful man, running down the road to marriage, serving God, raising a family. And somehow, in your mind it's all set to grand, glorious music. You have no idea how hard marriage can be! The times when you are completely misunderstood or cannot comprehend him (or do not want to). You also have no idea how wonderful marriage can be: sharing dreams, the warmth of love, being best friends, the incomparable joy of having children.

"You say your number-one desire is to follow God wholeheartedly. That's good. But there is no way to describe the conflicts that will burn inside of you. The challenge of making choices at every crossroad. Career choices. Spiritual choices. You can't see the giants in the Promised Land you're so eagerly entering. Now, your giants are 'Finances' and 'Opportunity.' But the real giants you must conquer will not be as obvious. They are inside you: negative attitudes, self-centeredness, pride, low self-esteem. But if you are aware of them, you can make life-long choices to conquer them."

I remember an altar in a small chapel on that same campus where, 25 years ago, I gave my life to Christ. It was the first of many altars in life: marriage, work, motherhood, loss. In each new place in life I have seen the necessity of making Jesus Lord, though at times with reluctance.

I recall a Sunday last winter. It was the final day of our prison conference in the women's penitentiary. We were having a communion service. I studied the faces of the women inmates—my new friends, some of them fellow believers…Marcia…Bea…Constance. Life had not been kind to them. Poor choices had brought most of them to this place. But now here in the presence of Jesus, we were on the same level, receiving grace and hope to go on. Many of the "props" that typically help define us—our address, occupation, family—had been taken from them. They had only a name, number, and blue uniform. I watched their wholehearted response to God and thought, *I, too, must come to Him, with no pretenses and nothing to prove.*

I am called upon in midlife to be wise and strong for everyone else: almost-grown children as they leave, aging parents, my husband. And he has his own giants to conquer: the community, church, and schools. But at past altars I have found—like Marcia, Bea, and Constance—that only a few choices are really important. The choice to keep learning from the Word, to keep growing. The choice to say "yes" to God, even in places of disillusionment and loss. The choice to make Jesus Lord of every new challenge—the most important choice we can ever make.

The choices we make shape our lives, some with more impact than others. How essential it is to make good choices! Reflect on your walk with God, beginning when you first came to Him. If you have a prayer journal, look through it for clues to your spiritual growth. Record ways you have changed. What important choices have you made that have made your life what it is today? What kind of choices can you make now that will improve your life?

Prayer

Lord, I thank You that You are merciful and faithful, and that You lead us step-by-step. Often our choices are self-serving and shortsighted, but You never fail to meet us with open arms whenever we turn to You. Teach us what it means to make choices that honor You—that help us build a life that honors You and makes a lasting impact for the kingdom.

"The only thing I can give to God is 'my right to myself.' If I will give God that, He will make a holy experiment out of me, and God's experiments always succeed."

—Oswald Chambers

19

Back to School

Grow in the grace and knowledge of
our Lord and Savior Jesus Christ.

2 PETER 3:18

When I was in school, fall was my favorite season. The warm, sunny days and crisp nights were energizing, and the challenge of new classes and new opportunities always made it seem like the beginning of wonderful things. But now autumn tends to make me sad, wistful. Maybe it's because when my children were small they went back to school, and carefree days of summer were over. The autumn-emotion deepened when they began leaving home.

Just recently I stood in the driveway watching Andy pull out, his little beat-up Nissan loaded as he headed back to college for the third time. I'd hugged his tall, lanky frame several times, trying to swallow a big lump in my throat. I knew he was eager to leave, but I would miss him so. I overheard Amy telling her friend, "My brother Andrew is such a sweetheart." His things were packed in so tightly that I worried he couldn't see out his back window. "Watch out for the other guy," I couldn't help advising. "I *am* the other guy," he deadpanned as he drove out of the driveway, not looking back. I could see that home was growing more distant to him now, his parents less necessary to his existence.

I immediately left for my walk, savoring the beauty of the newly turned aspen leaves against the blue sky. As I walked, I wiped away tears. "Why do those I love leave?" I asked no one in particular. I knew from watching Andy's three older brothers that this is the way it should be, but somehow that knowledge didn't help. As I walked, I was aware of the old familiar feelings of loss. I'd felt it recently in the midst of new joy, sharply reminded that I could never tell my parents—who had both passed away—that I would be a grandmother.

Change. It's inevitable, but it seems all I do now in life is let go—of people, expectations, and dreams. Why couldn't I be happy for Andy? I blew my nose and trudged down the path, reminded of a woman I once knew who was so disciplined to positive thinking that regardless of what happened, she praised God for it. *I should be more like her,* I thought, in awe of her perpetual spiritual cheerfulness.

Years ago, when Bill and I had two small children, I vividly remember one morning when my little duplex kitchen counter became a holy altar as I vowed to God, *"As long as I live, I will never stop learning, regardless of what You bring my way."* That was one of the most important promises I ever made. Also the most difficult because

I didn't know then that loss and change would often be my school. They still are. I am trying to learn to embrace these places, not run from them. And yet I didn't want to fall down into the hole of depression by seeing loss, as I'd once done. I knew I needed to have a disciplined mind—to see the positive, not always the negative. After all, God redeems the mind as well as the heart, the soul, and the body.

Having a disciplined mind doesn't mean mindlessly praising God for every bad thing that happens. The truth is, I live in a world of trouble and change as well as hope and beauty. Life is a mixed bag. I must remember that the mind is a powerful agent that affects everything, and it needs discipline—more at times than others. If I'm not diligent, fear, regret, and depression can hammer away at my mind, like a barking dog nips at my heels on a walk. Training my mind is like putting a dog through obedience school—she needs to learn to *stay*. Loving God with all my mind requires bringing my thoughts under His jurisdiction, praising Him in the midst of uncertainty, and thinking on things that are good, lovely, and pure. Isaiah says peace comes when our minds are *stayed* on Him (Isaiah 26:3). It takes a deliberate thought process to "set [my] mind on things above, not on things on the earth," as Colossians 3:2 says.

I came back from my walk that day and resolutely stripped Andy's bed to make his room habitable for company. I thought ahead to new projects, new challenges. I thanked God for the wonderful summer...and now a new season with new challenges.

What kind of season are you in, and are you ready to grow in your mind? Sometimes it's hard to see new opportunities for growth, but they are there if we will open our eyes and keep learning. Here are some Scriptures that can help us grow in our thinking:

Our minds need to be

- *disciplined to be stayed on God* (Isaiah 26:3)

- *thinking on good things* (Philippians 4:8)

- *humble* (Acts 20:19; Colossians 3:12)

- *renewed* (Romans 12:2; Ephesians 4:23)

- *sound* (2 Timothy 1:7)

- *sober* (Titus 2:6)

- *focused (versus double-minded)* (James 1:8)

Prayer

Lord, thank You for new things that come our way. Help us see in them the opportunity to grow and stretch our thinking. Thank you for the uncomfortable places that challenge us, that help us dig down deep to know what—and in Whom—we believe. More than anything, though, may we have the mind of Christ, to identify with You. In Jesus' name, amen.

More about Jesus let me learn,
More of His holy will discern;
Spirit of God, my teacher be,
Showing the things of Christ to me.

More, more about Jesus,
More, more about Jesus;
More of His saving fullness see,
More of His love Who died for me.
—ELIZA E. HEWITT

20

What Good Is Waiting?

Wait on the LORD; be of good courage, and He shall strengthen your heart; wait, I say, on the LORD!

PSALM 27:14

I was finally packed, prepared to leave for a speaking engagement that sunny winter Friday. Although lots of snow was on the ground, a tease of spring was in the air. I kissed Bill goodbye and set out on the two-and-a-half-hour drive that would take me over a mountain pass.

Or so I thought. As I rounded a curve, suddenly traffic slowed, then stopped. Trucks, cars, buses—everything stopped. I called Bill on the cell phone. He checked the Internet and found there was a snow slide covering the highway. Nobody was going anywhere for at least two hours. Two hours! My first thought was, *Thank goodness I brought some water!* My next thought was, *Oops, there are no bathrooms up here.* Well, all I could do was wait. And wait.

The high school kids on their way to a basketball game in the bus ahead got out and began throwing snowballs, having fun. The man behind me, whom I could see plainly in my rearview mirror, had the biggest scowl on his face—no doubt late for something important. A few adventurous souls who thought there had to be a shortcut zipped around the rest of us, which didn't go over too well with those who were waiting in line. But even they couldn't get far and eventually stopped. A few impatient people kept revving their engines, as if that would help. It was a classic study in how differently people *wait*.

I was tempted to take a nap but decided not to, in case traffic started moving. I didn't want to be left behind! I finally dug out my speaking notes and, wouldn't you know, one of the sessions I was teaching was on what it means to "wait on the Lord." I laughed aloud because I confess I find it hard to wait. Waiting often feels like wasted time to me—even the microwave sometimes seems too slow! And yet God tells us to wait on Him.

We can learn from Mary, the mother of Jesus, about what it means to wait. Much of her life was spent waiting. She spent time with her cousin Elizabeth waiting for Jesus to be born. After Jesus was born, she waited as she watched Him grow, wondering at her amazing son. After His ministry began, she waited as she watched it develop. At the crucifixion, she waited at the foot of the cross. She waited at the tomb. After Jesus ascended to heaven, she waited in the upper room with other believers—50 days!—for the promised gift of the Holy Spirit.

How wonderful it must have been for Mary to see the Holy Spirit poured out at Pentecost and to be in the midst of the excitement as the church began. All those years of wondering and waiting now came into focus. Her waiting had not been idleness—it was an active waiting. As she waited, she attended to family needs and went to weddings. She was submissive to God, and she trusted, even though the whole picture may not have been clear.

We too can wait with an active waiting. As I look back over the last ten years of my attempts to wait on God, I realize I still have a lot to learn, but I'm finding that waiting on God in our fast-paced world is absolutely essential and even beneficial:

Waiting helps you notice. If you ever have to wait an hour or two in an airport or mall, you begin to notice things. Before, you are primarily focused on your own agenda. But when you stop and wait, you see things you wouldn't have noticed previously. I never would have noticed all the people around me in traffic unless we had stopped for two hours on a mountainside. We can be so goal-oriented that we don't see people or see Him. Waiting on God is an inner waiting—to see with His eyes, to read Scripture with an open mind and heart. Sometimes waiting does mean to stop, to pause. But waiting on God isn't an empty waiting; it's an expectant waiting, a waiting for the Holy Spirit to birth something wonderful. "My eyes are ever on the LORD" (Psalm 25:15 NIV).

Waiting teaches trust. When we wait, our eyes are on the Lord. Not our problem, not our need—but on the Lord. When we wait for Him, we don't wait alone; He is there, even though He may be silent. "Waiting" means to not be in control...but rather to know that He is. It's a time to remember this: God has never failed us; He won't fail us now.

Are you in a place of waiting on God? Or perhaps you are aware that He is calling you to wait on Him to teach you fresh lessons of trust. Remember that waiting on God is the most efficient use of time there is, because when we wait on Him, we adjust our hearts to His purpose. It really is true that "those who wait on the LORD will find new strength. They will fly high on wings like eagles. They will run and not grow weary. They will walk and not faint" (Isaiah 40:31 NLT).

Prayer

Thank You, Lord, for showing us the importance of waiting on You. Remind us that "waiting" on You means to simply abide in Your presence with an open and submissive spirit, knowing You are at work. We wait with expectancy and with faith, knowing that all of Your ways are good. In Christ's name, amen.

How to Wait on God
"Before you pray, bow quietly before God, and seek to remember and realize who He is, how near He is, how certainly He can and will help.

"Just be still before Him, and allow His Holy Spirit to waken and stir up in your soul the child-like disposition of absolute dependence and confident expectation.

"Wait upon God as a Living Being, as the Living God, who notices you, and is just longing to fill you with His salvation.

"Wait on God till you know you have met Him; prayer will then become so different...Let there be intervals of silence, reverent stillness of soul, in which you yield yourself to God, in case He may have aught He wishes to teach you or to work in you.

"Waiting on Him will become the most blessed part of prayer, and the blessing thus obtained will be doubly precious as the fruit of such fellowship with the Holy One."

—Andrew Murray, *Waiting on God*

21

Best Friends with Jesus

"I have called you friends."

Jesus, in JOHN 15:15 NIV

When our son Eric was three, he was the middle child. Jon was a couple of years older, and Chris was the baby. We had recently moved, leaving behind all that was familiar to Eric—except Charlie Beakey, Eric's imaginary friend, who stuck with him through thick and thin. Charlie was an ideal friend—he never argued, he played whatever Eric wanted to play, and he was always there for Eric. After a year or two, though, Eric replaced Charlie Beakey with real friends.

Unfortunately, real people aren't perfect. This week I had a long discussion with our daughter, Amy—now a freshman in high school—about her current friendships, which seem quite complicated. I was tempted to give her some flip advice, such as "Oh, get over it!" when I remembered my own early teen years. I had a best friend through childhood. We took turns spending the night at each others' houses. We shared secrets. We pledged our undying loyalty and promised to be in each other's weddings. But when we reached high school, things changed. Our interests took us in different directions, and we made new friends. For some time, I had a sense of loss over the change in our best-friend status, and although we said hello to each other in the hallway, we never were best friends again.

My friends are precious to me. I *need* them, and I want to take good care of my friendships, even though there have been times when I haven't been there for my friends as I should have been. (I've been known to be so late with birthday cards that the recipient thought I was early.) But my friends are forgiving and faithful, and I am humbly grateful.

After all, there is only one perfect Friend. As I read John chapters 13 through 17, I find Jesus giving an amazing description of His disciples during their meal in the upper room just before He was crucified. What a ragtag bunch Jesus' disciples were! And yet He spent three years eating and sleeping and being with them and pouring His life into them. The Passover scene is especially poignant. *"You are My friends,"* He told them, as He washed their feet, prayed for them, and broke bread with them.

Judas, who betrayed the Lord for 30 pieces of silver, was also part of the group. Of course, I would expect bad things from Judas. But the rest of the disciples—how could they have been so unfaithful? In the Garden of Gethsemane, Jesus asked them to watch and pray. But in the hours of Jesus' greatest agony, while He wrestled with the realities of the cup His Father had prepared for Him, His friends didn't come through. *"Could you not keep watch for one hour?"* Jesus asked them (Mark 14:37 NIV).

I can understand the disciples' fear. They didn't want to get the same treatment Jesus got—and it certainly seemed possible, with the ugly mood of the crowd and the Roman officers. How was it, though, that these men who'd followed Him night and day and pledged their undying loyalty could go from discussing lofty eternal truths to falling apart when He needed them the most? To not even be able to stay awake and pray?

I like to think I would have been there for Jesus. That I wouldn't have panicked, that I wouldn't have been petty. That I would have prayed with Him in His great agony, even if I didn't understand what was going on.

But I'm afraid I'm one of the ragtag bunch myself. I can sit around and discuss spiritual things, pretend to have it all together—then when my back is against the wall, I'm thinking of my own skin. Intercessory prayer? I try. But it's not very glamorous. I can get serious about prayer when it's *my* needs. But if it's for the body of Christ at large, or someone I don't know very well, I am not so moved to pray. Fasting is hard for me. And if someone's need to be served inconveniences me, I can get evasive, busy. Like the disciples, my intentions are good, but I'm not always there for Jesus.

Jesus never fails us, though. Never. He loves us where we are, but He also sees what we can be. He is the best Friend anyone could have, and He is real, not a figment of our imagination. The friendship Jesus offers is not one to take lightly. It cost Him His very life. It is a holy, exclusive relationship, a best-friend relationship. And the more we know Him, the more we can honor Him by being a friend to those He places in our lives.

Do you need a friend? Try this: Be the kind of friend to someone else that you yourself would like to have. True friendship takes time—it takes opening up, allowing others into our lives and sharing in theirs, and going the extra mile with a person who needs someone to help carry the load. Jesus sacrificed His very life to be our Friend. If we are to know true friendship with others, we must follow Jesus' example of sacrifice. It's not easy, but the rewards are worth it.

Prayer

Lord, You created us with a capacity for friendship— and how we need it in life's ebbs and flows! May we learn from Your example how to be a real friend: to be inconvenienced, to care about what our friend is going through, to be there for her. Life can be lonely and hard. Thank You for being a best friend to us by giving Your very life—the greatest test of friendship ever. And, Lord, may I show by my life that I want to be Your friend, too. In Your name, amen.

Jesus! what a Friend for sinners!
Jesus! Lover of my soul;
Friends may fail me, foes assail me,
He, my Savior, makes me whole.

Hallelujah! what a Savior!
Hallelujah! what a Friend!
Saving, helping, keeping, loving,
He is with me to the end.
—J. WILBUR CHAPMAN

22

Time for Wisdom

*A man's days resemble grass. He blossoms like a
flower in the field, the wind blows over it, and it is
gone, with not a sign that it has been there. But the
LORD's faithful love rests eternally upon those who
revere Him, and His righteousness on the children's
children, on those who are faithful to His covenant,
who remember to carry out His instructions.*

I sit by Mother's bed, knowing she is leaving us. *There
is something very familiar about this,* I think. It seems in
many ways like a birth. Pain, uncertainty, travail.
Knowing her departure is imminent, yet not knowing
when. But, even here on this ordinary day while she is
dying, there is beauty, comfort, and routine. The sun is
shining brilliantly, and I sip a freshly brewed cup of coffee
as I watch her sleep. Through the open window, I hear
a family next door having dinner in their backyard, and
smell their barbecue. The ordinary business of living goes
on despite our business of dying.

Moments before, when I walked into her room, she
opened her brown eyes in alarm, worried about the
time—as she often does after she's been asleep. "What
time is it?" she asked. "I have to get going!" A habit, after
years of practice in catching a quick nap on the couch

while dinner was cooking, or a little rest on Sunday afternoon between church and meals. I help her to the bathroom—one of the last times she will be up. As always,
she is glad to see me. She loves having any of her family
close by. She loves us fiercely, insatiably. Exhausted by
the effort of walking, she sits back on her bed, and I hold
her upright. She leans into me, a slight smile on her face,
content just to be close. She takes a few sips of juice at
my coaxing, almost too weak to get the liquid into the
straw.

*What time is it, Mother...*My mind wanders. This is
the woman who used to awaken my sisters and me by
bursting into our room in the morning, inappropriately
cheerful (we thought), and quoting, *"Dost thou love life?*
Then do not waste time, for that is the stuff of which life is
made!" We'd groan and roll over, covering our heads with
our pillows.

Now she slips into a deep, dreamless sleep again. I
ease her thin frame back onto her bed. She seems stiff,
unable to readily get into a comfortable position. There
never is a good time for dying. And it's not easy letting
her go, even though we pray for her release. Days seem
like years as we keep vigil near her bedside, and we children come and go, watching her decline hourly.

In those final days, there are some sweet moments—
some smiles, even laughter. But watching her die, and
trying to make her comfortable as she leaves us, is
wrenching. Once after a horrendous night, the fog clears
from her mind, and she whispers to me, "You must be

pretty tired…You'd better go to bed." For a brief moment, she is "Mother" again.

Finally, the struggle was over, and time, as she knew it—minutes, days, months, years—stopped. Ten 'til five on a Tuesday morning, my sister, who was doing night duty, called me: "Mom's with Jesus…" I got there in just a few minutes and knelt by her bed, and cradled her little frame that was still warm…but so still, and growing cold. And so that week we made the trek back to Montana for her final reunion here on earth, laying her beside Dad under the headstone that reads, *"Till He Comes…"*

Now the flowers have wilted, the families have all gone home, and everyone is back to their routines. The month disrupted, I fuss with my calendar, rescheduling appointments, re-examining commitments. *"What time is it? I have to get going…"* Mother's words echo in my mind. Going? I suppose I have to "get going"—but where? To what?

I read in Psalm 90: *"We finish our years like a sigh…it is soon cut off, and we fly away…So teach us to number our days, that we may gain a heart of wisdom"* (verses 9-10,12). Wisdom means to understand what is true, right, and lasting. Watching my mother's death confronts me with my own mortality, and now it seems important that I not waste my life, not waste time.

I think of Mother's life now as a finished tapestry, a completed portrait. There are dark places in the picture…but overall, the dark places add depth and meaning to a portrait of a woman with a quest to know God, with a hunger for His Word. I watched her as she grew into a woman of wisdom, of gentle graces. As she leaned hard on God, listening for His still, small voice, studying His Word, she lived out her life for her family and those around her with humor and charm. My mother was a great woman, but I know she was convinced she had a great Savior.

Now as I ponder my calendar...my time...I pray with renewed desire, "Lord, I want to hear Your Word, live Your Word. This must be my priority. Teach me to apply my heart to wisdom." I know that "wisdom" takes time. It's a process of waiting, studying, listening—looking for the big picture to fulfill the purpose for our lives that God has for each of us.

Prayerfully consider your own life now. Is the way you are spending your time taking you toward a life of wisdom? We are all given the gift of our lives—this portion of time—and how we spend it is up to us. Scripture says, "Wisdom is the principal thing; therefore get wisdom. And in all your getting, get understanding" (Proverbs 4:7).

Prayer

I pray, Lord, that we will incline our hearts to You, to learn to walk in wisdom. May we spend our days and minutes wisely, not just busily, that we may redeem the time You have given us. And someday, when we are in Your presence, we will hear you say, "Well done, good and faithful servant!" In Christ's name, amen.

"Christianity is Christ living in us, and Christ has conquered everything…His love is so much stronger than death that the death of a Christian is a kind of triumph. And although we rightly sorrow…we rejoice in their death because it proves to us the strength of our mutual love. This is our great inheritance…this grip of clean love that holds us so fast that it keeps us eternally free. This love, this life, this presence, is the witness that the spirit of Christ lives in us, and that we belong to Him, and that the Father has given us to Him, and no man shall snatch us out of His hand."

—Thomas Merton, *No Man Is an Island*

23

Food from My Garden

Jesus said to Simon Peter, "Simon, son of John, do you love Me more than these?" He said to Him, "Yes, Lord; You know that I love You." He said to him, "Feed My lambs."

JOHN 21:15

Although for now I must be content with hanging baskets that can survive our transient schedule and short growing season, each year in the gentle warmth of spring I have a fleeting desire to have a garden. I have such good memories of our garden on the farm in Montana, my grandmother's project. She came out to the farm every weekend in the spring, and on Saturday mornings, she awakened us children with the promise of pancakes in order to enlist our help with her garden.

Dressed in Dad's bib overalls (I never dreamed then that her fashion sense was 40 years ahead of time), she would lead us out to weed and water. We knew how good the corn on the cob and string beans would taste later in the summer.

Perhaps someday we will live where I can have a garden and grow wonderful produce for the family. When everyone in our family is home, I need a full refrigerator and pantry. I always know when Andy is home from college because the cereal boxes get emptied. But often it's just Bill and Amy and me, and we don't need much. "How long has this been in here?" Bill asks as he scrutinizes the expiration date on a box.

Cleaning out my refrigerator, freezer, and pantry can be like an archaeological dig, the layers telling of events and months. When we lived in the Willamette Valley and fruit was abundant, I canned everything I could get my hands on. The other day I found a jar of plums from that era on the back of the top shelf, so old there wasn't even an expiration date. So I threw them out, saving the jar. We all agree on one thing—we want *fresh*. Fresh, tasty, nutritious food—good for the body.

At a speaking engagement in California, I met a young woman just out of college. An aspiring writer, she was frustrated at not getting published. I read some of her writing and tried to give her suggestions. I empathized with her, remembering how hard I worked at writing when I was her age, with little reward. Every time I sent an article to a publisher I prayed for acceptance, but often the manuscript came back. My burning desire was to connect with people, to communicate truth. I wanted to feed people with my words, my stories, but I didn't understand that my message wasn't fully developed yet. It has taken me years to see that my life is my real work—my real garden. And like a fruitful garden, my life has seasons: preparing the soil...planting the seed...watering...

weeding...and waiting—before I can produce anything that will feed people.

We nurturers all long to feed people, to encourage and love them with real truth. But how do we do that? How do we provide something fresh, nourishing, and life-giving that will point people to Christ? (When I was very small, I heard a preacher pray before he spoke, "And hide Thy servant behind the cross..." I peeked at him, wondering how he could hide behind the cross, because the cross in front was very skinny and was nailed to the wall.)

After Jesus' death and resurrection, He taught Peter and several other disciples a lesson about true ministry. They had decided to go fishing but had not caught any fish. After the disciples (except John) had abandoned Jesus in His hour of greatest need, no one would have blamed Him for scolding them. But instead, He helped them bring in a huge catch and then cooked fish for their breakfast by the sea.

There is an intriguing interchange between Jesus and Peter. Three times Jesus asked Peter, "Peter, do you love Me?" Each time, Peter answered Him, "Yes, Lord, You know that I love You." Jesus told him, "Feed My lambs... tend My sheep...feed My sheep."

I wonder a lot about this passage. What does it take to truly follow Jesus, to "feed" others out of what He is doing in my life? There are times when I think I am finished, and I'm tempted to just go fishing. But Jesus asks gently, "Do you love Me? Then feed My sheep."

A friend of mine is enduring unbelievable testing. God has used her greatly in the past, but now she is in a time of confusion and pain. As I watch her in this crucible, I truly believe that out of this season will come new growth and insights by which she will again nourish people in a powerful, fresh way. She is literally being hidden by the cross of suffering, but there will be fruit from this season. I believe that, because her heart is open to God—even now when she doesn't have any answers.

So many of us desperately need to be fed from God, asking inwardly, as Walter Brueggemann put it, "Is there a word from the Lord that will help me live? Is there a word to rescue me from my exhausted coping?" Yes, there is, and the word is this: *God loves us*. That is a magnificent truth that Jesus died for, and in order for this truth to be palatable to others from our lives, it must not be stale. We must be living and experiencing it now.

Fruit develops in us as we stay "in the vine," go through seasons with Him, invite His presence deep into our lives, be honest about what's there. If we do not gain nourishment from Him, we cannot feed others. It is when He feeds our hearts that we have something to give others—something real, fresh, and nourishing.

Prayer

Lord, it isn't enough to give out of stale experiences, out of long-past victories and successes. We confess our need and our utter dependence on You to do a fresh work of grace in our lives. May we be up-to-date in our experience with You—in touch with what You are doing in our lives now—so that what we give to others is real and palatable. In Jesus' name, amen.

"The people who are of absolutely no use to God are those who have sat down and have become overgrown with spiritual mildew; all they can do is to refer to an experience they had twenty or thirty years ago. That is of no use whatever, we must be vitally at it all the time. With Paul it was never 'an experience I once had,' but 'the life which I now live.'"

—Oswald Chambers, from *Oswald Chambers:*
The Best from All His Books

24

Living Life's Parentheses

I want you to know, dear brothers and sisters, that everything that has happened to me here has helped to spread the Good News. For everyone here, including all the soldiers in the palace guard, knows that I am in chains because of Christ. And because of my imprisonment, many of the Christians here have gained confidence and become more bold in telling others about Christ.

PHILIPPIANS 1:12-14 NLT

It was Sunday, and we were on our way home from church. I was looking forward to leisure time, reading the Sunday paper and then painting the railing in the family room. We were doing a major remodeling of our house, and it seemed as if it would never end. *If we could do just one thing a day,* I reasoned, *it would help.* Today I was going to tackle that railing.

Chris broke into my thoughts. "Mom, see those bluffs over there? I've heard that's a great hike. Let's pack our lunch and go up there."

"Well, I was going to paint, but..." The eager look on his face weakened my resolve. "Let's go!"

It was a late spring afternoon, the sun warm and the air sweet with the scent of wildflowers. We hurriedly changed clothes, packed our backpacks with sandwiches, drinks, the Sunday paper, and a book on Hemingway

(Chris had a paper due the next day), and drove off toward the bluffs. Chris parked the car on the side of a little-traveled dirt road, and we set off on a trail through the manzanita bushes and ponderosa pines, winding our way up the bluff.

"Chris! Do you know where you're going?"

He was way ahead of me on the trail, his slender form stooped with his backpack, blond hair glinting in the sunlight. The trail grew steeper, and the hike turned into a climb. Before long we reached the top, breathless yet exhilarated.

"There!" Chris turned to me triumphantly. "I thought this was what we'd see!"

I caught my breath. Stretched far below was a vast green meadow with a river winding through it. Glistening snow-capped peaks towered above where hawks and eagles soared on the wind. How often had I driven past these bluffs, never dreaming that this was behind them?

"Chris..." He was busy spreading out towels on the warm rocks and arranging our lunch so we would have the best view.

"Yeah, Mom?"

How often had I looked at him—my third son—and not seen all the wonder and beauty? How do you tell your 17-year-old how much you love him? How do you express the heart-stopping realization, *My child, you are almost an adult...and you're wonderful!* Instead I said, "Thanks, honey, for bringing me up here."

We ate our lunch in the sun, and Chris and I talked about the future, his interests, his world. That sunny

Sunday afternoon was unexpected and unplanned. But the memory of talking with my son, high on a rocky bluff, is one I will always cherish.

My mind flashed back three years further, to when our magazine staff was rapidly expanding. Those were exciting, exhausting days: designing layout, exploring demographics, interviewing and hiring new staff. One day an elderly woman with a cane came in the door.

She announced that she would like to see our offices and then talk to someone about the magazines. Everyone else seemed busy, so I reluctantly gave her a tour. When we finished, I took her to my office, and she sat down heavily in a chair.

"Can't walk like I used to. I had a friend drive me here," she explained. "While I was praying the other day, the Lord laid these magazines on my mind. Is it all right if I pray for them?"

Was it *all right?* We joined hands, and Flora prayed for my husband, the editors, the assistants and artists; those in circulation and advertising; the writers and the readers. Flora's simple prayer brought all of us immeasurable encouragement at just the right time. What I first perceived as an interruption was really a very needed affirmation that God's hand was on what we were doing.

It's mysterious the way God moves in our lives. Often the "real event" is not on the calendar. It just happens—like a happening within a happening. These are life's "parentheses"—which become the real agenda.

Have there been "parentheses" in your life—unplanned, unexpected occurrences? Mark 5:24-34 tells of the chronically ill woman who made her way through the crowd to touch Jesus. She said, "If only I may touch His clothes, I shall be made well." This woman was an interruption to Jesus. He was on His way to minister to someone else, and this woman was not a scheduled stop on the way. Yet what happened when He responded to the interruption became an important faith-inspiring story recorded for us in Scripture.

Prayerfully consider what you can learn from the way Jesus lived. He spent his earthly life responding to interruptions and people's needs. Ask Jesus to open your eyes to interruptions that may really be divine appointments. And maybe, as I did that day on the high bluff with Chris, and the day that Flora came to visit our magazine office, you can hear God speaking to you there.

Prayer

Thank You, Lord, for intruding into our lives to show us what is truly important. Sometimes we're so focused on our own agenda that we fail to see You in the unexpected and uninvited interruptions in our lives. Father, we ask You to speak to us, however You will. We only pray that we will have the grace and wisdom to see You and hear You in the "parentheses" of life, and that we will come away gladly to learn from You in those times. In Jesus' name, amen.

"The great thing, if one can, is to stop regarding all the unpleasant things as interruptions of one's 'own' or 'real' life. The truth is of course that what one calls the interruptions are precisely one's real life—the life God is sending one day by day: what one calls one's 'real life' is a phantom of one's own imagination."

—C.S. Lewis, *The Letters of C.S. Lewis*
to Arthur Greeves

25

The Power of Words

Let the words of my mouth and the meditation
of my heart be acceptable in Your sight, O LORD,
my strength and my Redeemer.

PSALM 19:14

Oh, the agony and the joy of words! How they fail me, yet how I pursue the challenge of trying to capture with words an emotion, a fleeting impression—or make sense of something. Words can immortalize a sliver of life before it is forever lost and capture something beautiful or significant.

Writing is one way to do this. However, spontaneous words from my mouth are quite another. It's hard to edit words already spoken. My words have gotten me in trouble. I have said and spoken and used *so many words*—probably more than my share! I've said things I've regretted. And there are times I should have spoken and didn't. I've used words to share God's love...and at times used them to cause resentment. For instance, years ago while speaking on family issues, I boldly stated that if a parent simply did such-and-such, she would never have to worry about her child's behavior. After the meeting,

125

a woman approached me, insisting tearfully, "But I did that, and my son still rebelled." I remember thinking if that lady would just get her act together, she wouldn't have those problems. I was *so sure*. But now, after years of experience, I realize my words brought a burden of judgment to a struggling mother. How I wish I could take back those words and help restore the passion for parenting to that woman.

Why do we say the things we say? I think it is often because we have hidden agendas with our words—perhaps even hidden to us. Words come out of our *intent* toward others and reflect the condition of our hearts. With words, we can extend to others good will or evil. We can instruct or demand. We can express anger or passion. We can tell the truth harshly or in a way to encourage and help ease someone's burden. But our words remind us how much we need Jesus to rule our hearts. It's not an overnight process, and it comforts me that James reminds us of the untamed tongue and that "out of the same mouth proceed blessing and cursing"—and admits that "we all stumble in many things." Indeed!

In Solomon's Temple there was a beautiful analogy of how we can restore one another. In order to keep the lamps burning brightly, the priest would trim the sputtering wick with golden tongs and then place the burned-out portion inside a golden covered dish so that no one saw the burned and ugly part. Only the beautiful, glowing lamp was seen, burning brightly for the glory of God (see 1 Kings 7). This speaks to me of using discretion in what we say about others: Do my words diminish or enhance the individual being discussed?

Some time ago, someone with inside information told me something negative about a musician who sang (until then) my favorite song. Somehow, the song wasn't the same for me after that. The truth is, I know something "bad" about everyone I know, including me. And while much of our conversation involves basic sharing of information, there is another level of information that carries a sting from the intent behind the words. As Larry Crabb writes, "Sometimes we just want to destroy the competition." We can kill with so few words. But we can invite life, too, by only a few words.

Once a friend pointed out to me a redeeming quality in a public figure who receives more than her share of criticism. I admit I have criticized her, too—far more than I've prayed for her. But now every time I hear criticism of this person, I am reminded of my friend's comment, and I'm more inclined to feel compassion. I doubt that my friend even remembers her simple, positive words. But I do. *Words are powerful.*

Perhaps the most power our words have is over our family members and close friends. One couple with a vibrant marriage of more than 30 years confided that every day they make it a point to say something positive to one another—and make a point to forgive the negative. Small words can have an enormous impact.

The words we say have an impact upon ourselves as well as on others. If you want to be understood, speak your truth in love (see Ephesians 4:25). Don't assume people know what you're going through. The words we say to others regarding other people are powerful as well.

Here are some simple, helpful rules: Before speaking, ask, *Is it true? Does it build up or tear down? Who or what is helped by my sharing this?*

George Herbert, a seventeenth-century preacher, wrote, "Good words are worth much, and cost little." Be they mundane or crafted, words have a powerful influence...and how important it is that our words bring blessing, and not pain.

Jesus' holy words burn like a fire, going straight to the intent of our hearts. But as purifying and truthful as His words are, they don't destroy—but convict, convert, and redeem.

Prayer

Lord, Your words have given me life! They set my soul on fire and their truth and love penetrate to the deepest part of my being. Your words comfort me, convict me...They guide me. As one created in Your image, You have given me the use of words—of creating relationships. I pray that my life will be so immersed in *Your* words that *my* words will bring Your grace and healing to others. In Jesus' name, amen.

"There is a grace of kind listening, as well as a grace of kind speaking...Kind words are the music of the world. They have a power which seems to be beyond natural causes, as though they were some angel's song which had lost its way and came to earth."

—Frederick William Faber (1814-1863)

26

Convinced of Grace

By grace you have been saved through faith, and that not of yourselves; it is the gift of God, not of works, lest anyone should boast.

EPHESIANS 2:8-9

I like things *nice.* Nicely decorated house, nice children, nice husband. And I try to be nice, too. Maybe it's a carry-over from my childhood. When I was active in 4-H, the phrase "make the best better" was drilled into my head. And behavior and appearances were important to my family.

One day as I left home to go to a dress-up function at school, my mother checked me over before I went out the door. I'd worked hard to look as good as an awkward 13-year-old can look. She smiled her approval, then said, "Wait—your shoes need polishing. You should look perfect from head to toe!"

The pursuit of excellence I learned as a child propels me to do the best job I can to be a good wife and mother. This pursuit becomes dangerous, though, when things become more important than people. And such a narrowed focus can be especially deadly in the spiritual realm.

Last Sunday afternoon while everyone else in the house was busy, I slipped away for a walk. The sun was shining after a long absence, and the wind felt brisk. I slowed my pace, not so intent on the exercise as on enjoying the sun.

I looked for a spot out of the wind where the sun was shining just so, and sat down on a log at the edge of a meadow. As I soaked up the warm rays, I mulled over a hauntingly moving yet disturbing story I'd read a few days before in Luke chapter 7.

Jesus had been invited to the house of Simon, a Pharisee, for dinner. The meal was an elaborate affair, and as was their custom, the guests reclined on couches as they ate (my family would love that). In the home of this proper religious leader, a woman known to be a sinner intruded with an alabaster flask of fragrant ointment. In an almost embarrassing outpouring of worship and adoration, she began bathing Jesus' feet with her tears and the ointment, wiping His feet with her hair. The religious leaders frowned on this sensational, emotional display. But their disdain didn't bother her—she had nothing to lose. Jesus then changed her life as He offered her forgiveness.

The sun feels so good, I thought. Cradled by its warmth, I realized that before long, the deep blue of columbine and the vivid orange splashes of shooting stars would fill the meadow, blooming after a long winter. I thought about the woman at Jesus' feet, and how receiving grace from Jesus was like soaking in the sun. She just drank it in. W.H. Auden wrote, "It is where we are wounded that God speaks to us." Jesus spoke grace into this woman's deepest wounds and sin, and she was overcome and transformed by His grace.

After years of counseling people, Dr. David Seamands said he was convinced the basic cause of some of the most disturbing emotional–spiritual problems that trouble evangelical Christians is their failure to receive and live out God's unconditional grace—and the corresponding failure to offer that grace to others.

I admit I've found it hard to internalize God's grace. It's easier to do all the "right" things: attend church, witness when the occasion calls for it, take a moral stand on issues—all worthy pursuits. But if they're prompted by the desire to conform to some invisible code of "Christian correctness," my actions miss the mark of Christ's example.

Sometimes I look back over my own failings and agonize, *How could I have done that? How could I have said that? How could I have been so thoughtless?* Self-recrimination and self-condemnation signal my need to experience grace. Why should I be surprised at my shortcomings? Of course I fail. But I am receiving a fresh understanding of grace as I learn to welcome the humbling experiences in my life. I am learning to ask others for prayer, for forgiveness. To not be so "right" all the time. I'm learning I can't afford to judge others because that's God's business, not mine.

Do you feel you have an understanding of grace? Read the story in Luke 7 about the woman and ask yourself,

Who do I most identify with in this story? The woman, the disciples, or Simon the Pharisee? Consider how God has shown His grace to you in the past. What are ways you can actively receive His grace, and in turn give it to others?

Prayer ·

O God, thank You for Your abiding presence with us. Whatever the cost, may we dwell in Your presence, the ultimate safe place. Whether we feel Your presence or not, help us to trust what Your Word tells us about Your care for Your people. May we find comfort in the knowledge that You shelter us in the cleft of the rock and cover us with Your mighty hand. In Jesus' name, amen.

O to grace how great a debtor
Daily I'm constrained to be!
Let Thy goodness, like a fetter,
Bind my wandering heart to Thee.
—ROBERT ROBINSON

27

Trees of Righteousness

The righteous shall flourish like a palm tree, he shall grow like a cedar in Lebanon. Those who are planted in the house of the LORD shall flourish in the courts of our God. They shall still bear fruit in old age; they shall be fresh and flourishing.

PSALM 92:12-14

I sit with my morning coffee, looking out onto a frosty scene. Most mornings the sun fills this room, but this morning it's snowing a fine, steady stream of snow, so cold it seems the snow has to force its way down. This is a real January snow, not a Christmas-card one.

Directly out my dining room window stands a magnificent ponderosa pine we've been told is 200 years old or more. It has seen a lot under the central Oregon sky: forest fires...blustery springs...hot, dry summers... freezing winters. Most likely it was mute witness to Native Americans hunting deer, elk, and bear. Now it has the Carmichael family snuggled up next to it. And still it stands, impervious to all around it—lifting its elegant branches toward heaven.

I haven't seen as many seasons as our tree (although my daughter thinks I have), yet I, too, am affected by their passing. Now I am feeling keenly the effects of the emptying nest. I have experienced other seasons, too, that may be less obvious, but are just as real. I went through a season of idealism in my youth, when I lived mainly on hopes and dreams and nothing seemed impossible. Then I went through a season of invincibility when I was convinced that if I followed a certain formula, I would succeed.

Those earlier seasons were sunny, warm times when the world seemed right side up. Now, midlife seems to have its share of storms, often unpredictable and scary. The other day I listened to a friend who is having a crisis in her family, and I was again reminded that it rains on the just and the unjust. Sometimes things happen with no apparent explanation. She'd done it all "right," yet she is now in desperate need of God's intervention.

I have also experienced seasons of blessing when I've sensed God's presence so strongly it was almost tangible... times when my prayers are answered and I see God moving in our family, in our church, and around us. I like this rare kind of season best and tend to think, *Finally! This is how it should always be!* But it's not always that way.

Now I find myself in a season of *not knowing*, a most difficult place because I like to have loose ends tied up, and the editor in me wants a finished manuscript. But this is where I am learning important lessons of trust. Emerson wrote, "All I have seen teaches me to trust the Creator for all I have not seen." God's very nature is faithfulness, and He cannot deny Himself. Having to trust Him in a season of not knowing is an opportunity for my roots to go down deep, down where the nourishment is, to His Word, which is faithful and true.

What is His message to me in uncertainty? Simply that I must not cast away my confidence. There's a very still small voice that says, *"Trust Me. Put aside your striving, your manipulating, and simply trust Me."* It can be hard to listen to that voice when what I *see* is not faith-inspiring but fear-producing. These are perilous times for people of faith. Fellow believers in some parts of the world are facing persecution, even death, and we must pray for them, stand with them. Even our own culture is subtly but pervasively hostile to righteousness. If I trust what I see, I can become terrified for my children and grandchildren because the world is so strong, its messages so persistent. But Scripture says that God is able to keep that which I commit to Him. And I do commit my family to Him, believing for the best.

Somehow my father, trees, and Psalm 1 are all tied together in my mind because Dad, a righteous man, was *planted* in God: "Blessed is the man who walks not in the counsel of the ungodly, nor stands in the path of sinners, nor sits in the seat of the scornful; but his delight is in the law of the LORD, and in His law he meditates day and night. He shall be like a tree planted by the rivers of water, that brings forth its fruit in its season, whose leaf also shall not wither; and whatever he does shall prosper" (Psalm 1:1-3).

Shortly after my father died, Mother gave me a black-and-white snapshot of Dad holding me when I was two years old. I cherish that picture, as there is something infinitely precious about being held by one's father.

Being rooted and planted in God is like being held by Him. It provides the stability to survive difficult seasons and storms. As I look to the future, I have no idea what's ahead. For now, I am learning to trust. To be deeply rooted in God means we cling to Him when we think we understand—and especially when we don't—knowing He holds us and all that we commit to Him.

What kind of season are you in now? How are you responding to God there? Your response to Him is what can make your roots grow deep. It's not the circumstance so much as it is the response to it that makes the difference in the life of one whose trust is in the Lord. Don't give up, and don't be swayed by the negative things around you. It is possible for you to be planted in God and have a life that bears fruit. But it takes patience, persistence, and a lot of trusting in the character of God through all seasons of life.

Prayer

O God, as I change and grow—help me grow toward You. Let me not envy the one who may be planted elsewhere in life—or may be in a different season in his or her development. Only let me be faithful where You have me. May I put my roots down deep so that I will not be swayed or moved by what I see. Thank You for Your faithfulness—great is Your faithfulness! In Christ's name, amen.

"Real trust doesn't occur until we've committed the full weight of our hopes, dreams, and expectations—our very lives—into His hands."

—Ron Mehl, *The Cure for a Troubled Heart*

28

Leaving the Wilderness

To everything there is a season, a time for every purpose under heaven:…a time to break down, and a time to build up; a time to weep, and a time to laugh…

ECCLESIASTES 3:1-4

I was flying home from a speaking engagement. It was a clear, crisp day, the visibility unusually good. I leaned my head against the window, drinking in the view. I was tired, and it felt good to relax.

I thought of the people I had met on this trip. I had flown to a city on the other side of America, where I didn't know anyone. But during this short time, I had made some new friends. One woman in particular, a leader in her church and community, had made an impression on me. She had waited until everyone else had left after I finished speaking. Then she had crumpled as she poured out her heart about the difficulties she was going through. Often a speaker is a "safe place" to tell secrets. As I listened, I had been amazed again at the depth of pain in people's lives, the depth of their private agonies. I had been able to tell that in spite of her outwardly put-together life, this woman was experiencing the loneliness and pain

138

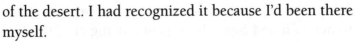

of the desert. I had recognized it because I'd been there myself.

I looked down again. We had passed the Plains and were now over the Great Basin—mile upon mile of wilderness. It appeared to be flat, dry, and barren. *What brave souls would want to live here?* I wondered. And then, surprisingly, I saw little communities, a solitary house at the end of a road here and there. I wanted to shout down to them, "Hey! Why do you stay there? Don't you know that only a thousand miles away are beautiful, fertile places, where things grow? Why settle here, where you're forced to eke out an existence? You just gotta get over those mountains...get out of that wilderness!" And I'm sure many of them would shout back, "Mind your own business—we like it here. It has its own beauty, you know!"

As I flew on, I thought of Hagar, Sarah's handmaiden. She had given birth to Abraham's son Ishmael. This was causing major problems and jealousies in the camp. Finally, Sarah insisted to Abraham that Hagar and Ishmael had to go (Genesis 21).

In the wilderness, when Hagar and Ishmael were at the point of desperation and death, God saw their plight and sustained them with water from a well. If we read further, Scripture tells us that Hagar *stayed* in the desert. She lived there, found a wife for Ishmael in Egypt, and died there. The Bible says that God was with Ishmael as he grew up in the wilderness.

As surely as there are times to go to the wilderness, there are also times to leave it and move on. How funny we humans are—we go kicking and screaming into the wilderness of pain or sickness—and then we grow accustomed to it and resist the idea of moving on. I think of Moses, escaping to the back side of the wilderness after he killed the Egyptian (Exodus 2). And Elijah, running to the desert to escape from Jezebel and Ahab (1 Kings 19). Jesus spent time in the wilderness preparing for His public ministry.

Some would avoid desert experiences at all cost—deny they exist, deny their validity. But desert experiences are valuable—indeed, they are an essential part of a fruitful life. We hear God's voice and He refreshes us while we are there. But the time will come—if we are committed to growth—when we will leave the wilderness.

Not long ago I went alone to a favorite spot in the mountains. I packed a small can of juice and some crackers in my jacket pocket and began to hike off the dirt road. The mountains stretched off in the distance, their snowcapped peaks against the blue sky, breathtaking in their beauty. I found an old tree stump. There I set out the crackers and the juice, sang a hymn of the cross, and had a private communion service. As I prayed, I considered a burden I'd often relinquished but had gone back and picked up once more. I was sensing it was time to "leave that wilderness." I wrote out the burden, rolled up the little piece of paper, and slipped it inside the tree stump. This time when I left it with Him, I didn't look back. Paul Tournier wrote, "Life and faith always insist on moving forward—and I cannot move forward without leaving something behind...and possibly the most difficult to let go are treasures of painful experiences."

When it is time to move on, it is time to be recon-
ciled to imperfections, time for forgiveness, time to stop
being a victim, time to take responsibility for where I am,
who I am. Time to stop being enamored by, consumed
by, the austere beauty of the desert. "Forgetting what is
behind... I press on" (Philippians 3:13-14 NIV).

And where do you move on to? To the place where
you can once again pick up the towel of servanthood,
risk following God, stretch your faith. Only this time you
move on armed with lessons you have learned in the
wilderness.

Have you spent time in the desert recently? Are you
there now? If so, what have you learned? Have you
learned the value of the desert? Prayerfully consider
whether it might be time for you to leave that place and
move on. It may help you to record the lessons you have
learned there and then write some "spiritual goals" for
yourself. Put them in a sealed envelope, and tuck them
away somewhere to be opened and reviewed at a later
date. Remember that spiritual growth may require preparation time in the desert, but it also requires that we
follow God's leading out of the desert and use what He
has taught us to encourage others.

Prayer
        Lord, our life is truly a pilgrimage with You!
Sometimes You lead us to beautiful, sunny places, and
sometimes to a desolate wilderness, where it's hard to
understand what You're doing. But Lord, we can trust
Your goodness. Give us courage to follow You out of the

desert and into new places of victory and provision. Keep us from becoming too comfortable in the desert...so that when You call us, we are ready to move. In Jesus' name, amen.

"What quickens my pulse now is the stretch ahead rather than the one behind, and it is mainly for some clue as to where I am going that I search through where I have been, for some hint as to who I am becoming or failing to become that I delve into what used to be."

—Frederick Buechner, *The Sacred Journey*

29

Life and Lists

Don't worry about having enough food or drink or clothing. Why be like the pagans who are so deeply concerned about these things? Your heavenly Father already knows all your needs, and he will give you all you need from day to day if you live for him and make the Kingdom of God your primary concern.

MATTHEW 6:31-33 NLT

Today is Monday, and this is my routine: first, a steaming mug of French roast; then a half hour or so of Bible study and prayer journaling. Finally I make The List for the week: phone calls, correspondence, meals, things needed at the store, work projects. Things to do. Some of the items on the list are left over from last week (last month, if I'm brutally honest).

I've found that The List is necessary, because if I don't write it down, I will forget it or not get it done. I won't stay focused. Farm girl that I am, I think of my list as a corral that keeps me from wandering off chasing butterflies, and then later wondering where the day went. The List keeps me on track, and I have a sense of satisfaction when I can cross something off.

But there are times—especially this morning—when it seems The List is too long, too demanding. I know, I know...I wrote it. But hovering over me is the thought that next week will bring another List, as necessary as my morning coffee.

I shouldn't resist the idea of lists—after all, it's simply a reflection of where I am in life. Recently I found a list I made 26 years ago, the day before our son Andy was born: *nursing pads, baby oil, disposable diapers.* Today my list for town is *prescription, antacid, decaffeinated coffee.* When cleaning out my oversized handbag, I found some old lists that told me about an event—who we had for dinner, what we were celebrating. A list can be a history of sorts.

It's important to know what to put on the list. And just because I list something doesn't mean I should. I've been known to be unrealistic in my list-making, such as the time I bought and prepared 100 pineapple boats for a women's luncheon while I had three little boys under five at my feet.

Today at the top of the list is, *Write a column that will help people (including me) grow in God.* To be honest, as I padded out to the kitchen today I didn't feel like making a list. I wanted to go on a hike along the river and look at wildflowers. But life does not consist of doing only things you feel like doing. Lists help carry out plans, and plans help shape a life. My husband, Bill, is a long-range planner. He started planning for retirement 25 years ago—a thought that disconcerted me, since I was still changing diapers. His lists back then have helped us now, though, and I'm grateful.

But the important thing about lists and plans is that they must be first of all submitted to God. There's a Short

List (meaning the list of things that really are important), which must provide the overall principles for everything else on our lists, principles such as loving Jesus with all our heart, soul, mind, and strength.

Do my weekly and daily lists reflect that Ultimate List? The writer of Proverbs says to trust Him in all ways...to acknowledge Him, and He will direct our paths (see 3:5-6). Paul told the Philippians that, when all was said and done, it was most important to "rejoice in the Lord" (Philippians 3:1). He went on to encourage us believers to not put our confidence in what we can do (what I can cross off my list), but in Whom we know. It seems that God's list has more to do with "being" than with "doing."

There is a sense of awe...and comfort, too...in knowing that the One who knows no time put aside His glorious garment of light to take on the human form in order to communicate redeeming love to us, His children. He owns our time, our days, our Mondays. Our lists. We plan the best we can, but when we are His, He can preempt any list. Indeed, as I look back, often the things that have been the most instructive and memorable are those that were not on the list...they just happened.

Tomorrow, I will hike along a river with some friends. We will look at God's incredible creation and talk of His faithfulness. Then I will come home and check this off my list: *Rejoice.*

Think about how you can invite Christ into the ordinary, commonplace moments of your day and "celebrate" His presence.

Prayer

     Lord, You came to redeem our entire life, to give us abundant, overflowing joy. We say we want Your joy, but often we cram our lives so full that we ask You to wait while we are occupied with other things. Forgive us, Lord. We do invite You—right now—into the moments of our lives. Show us what is most important in Your eyes. We want to obey You, Lord, to pour out what You give us so that others will be refreshed. In Jesus' name, amen.

"Joy is really a road sign pointing us to God. Once we have found God...we no longer need to trouble ourselves so much about the quest for joy."

—C.S. Lewis, *Surprised by Joy*

30

Following Jesus

*All those who want to be my disciples must come
and follow me, because my servants must be where
I am. And if they follow me, the Father will honor
them.*

JOHN 12:26 NLT

One spring when our children were small, I was helping
with vacation Bible school. My friend Sue and I were
responsible for recruiting volunteers. One afternoon at
a committee meeting Sue told me, "I called Pauline"—
a middle-aged woman—"to see if she could help us one
hour a day for five mornings, and she said, 'No, because
that's when I water my garden.'" Sue couldn't believe it.
"It wasn't an excuse!" she continued. "Pauline was
serious."

Sue and I stared at each other, open-mouthed. What
planet did that woman inhabit? I could not conceive of
such thinking. How could watering peas and beans be
more important than teaching children about God?

Now, 25 years later, I find myself in the unexpected
place of understanding Pauline. Maybe *being* like her.
What is at the heart of such thinking? It can be weariness

or ill health. Or maybe it's the same kind of thinking that prompted Peter to go back to fishing after Jesus was arrested and executed. Forget the ministry stuff—it's too crushing, too exhausting. And although it's hard to admit, sometimes we who work with people can become cynical. "I did all that—and look what happened. It's easier to invest in inanimate objects or things that can't talk back." Maybe that's why empty nesters get little dogs: They're cute, they don't break your heart, and they don't have souls to worry about.

Sometimes I ask myself, *Why do Bill and I keep doing marriage seminars? People who should know better still divorce each other. Why work with kids these days? Their world is too strange. Why travel to unfamiliar places, stay in lonely hotels, speak to people that you're not sure are wanting to change or grow?*

Discipleship can become more demanding—easier to resist and justify resisting—as we grow older. We know more. We've seen more. And while we may not be bitter, we can become more clever at avoiding Him and avoiding obedience.

Midlife can be a tempting season to "turn the needs off," to become complacent. I love being home with my books, my piano, my flowers, watching the sun stream through the windows on my gleaming wood floor. It's comfortable to spend time with my husband and family and friends—to read good books, take long walks. Reflect and think. These things give me great pleasure, and surely they are gifts from God.

And yes, they are…but let's be honest: Midlife can be a time of selfishness and laziness. We find it easier to avoid risks in order to stay comfortable. And I'm keenly aware that in this business of following Jesus, there's a fine balance. At one time in my life I "worked" so frenetically for Jesus that I became ill—before I finally understood that it was by grace I am saved, not by works.

But there is a cost to following Jesus, and obedience often is not convenient or easy. Otherwise, why would Jesus tell us to take up our crosses to follow Him? What is your cross, what is my cross? My cross is that I find it easier to love ideas than to love people. People can be very messy and inconvenient, not to mention sheer hard work.

Last year we were invited to speak at a family conference on the East Coast. I worked hard on my presentation, getting my notes just right. This family conference had a twist: They were families of inmates. It would be a challenge to address their needs.

After I checked into my room, I met my neighbor across the hall: Barbara, mother of four boys under five years of age. *Very* hyperactive boys, one of whom got sick in the middle of the night. As it turned out, that weekend Barbara and her sons adopted me as their "grandmom," and I spent most of the weekend sitting with her at mealtimes, making a midnight run to get medicine for her sick baby, talking to her, holding her little boys. When it came time to speak, I was so frazzled that my presentation was not polished. My back ached, I was tired, and my hair was a mess.

But on the Sunday we left, Barbara made a commitment to follow Jesus and brought her little boys to the altar to be dedicated in the morning worship service.

I flew home to Oregon, exhilarated to realize that God had used me, although not in the way I thought He was going to. But I'm beginning to understand that Jesus doesn't call us to be polished—He only calls us to be obedient, offering what we have and who we are. And at His touch, we can help build the Kingdom.

Prayer

Lord, thank You for reminding us that You have so much more for us if we will just have the courage to follow You. Forgive us for wanting to be safe and comfortable. Thank You for reminding us that we don't need to have everything all spelled out, that it's enough to follow You. Help us to trust that You know the way. May we diligently study Your Word and have the courage to engage the opportunities You place in our path. In Jesus' name, amen.

"There is a first faith and a second faith. The first faith is the easy, traditional belief of childhood, taken from other people, believed because it belongs to the time and land. The second faith is the personal conviction of the soul. It is the heart knowing, because God has spoken to it."

—Phillips Brooks, *Treasury of the Christian Faith*

31

Taking Inventory

Be watchful, and strengthen the things which remain.

REVELATION 3:2

These three remain: faith, hope and love. But the greatest of these is love.

1 CORINTHIANS 13:13 NIV

Even though it was still dark, I was suddenly wide awake. Trying not to disturb my husband's sleep, I put on my robe and slippers and went out to my "spot"—a loveseat near the bay window, where I usually have my coffee and quiet time. The woodstove still had embers glowing as I sat down with my Bible and notebook.

I realized why I was awake. *We were moving in three days.* How on earth was I going to get everything done? I had been packing for weeks—sorting, throwing, and giving things away. It was shocking to realize how much stuff we had crammed into one house after 23 years and five children. In the back of my closet, I had found a box of my wedding announcements (35 years old)! There were countless things from my children—notebooks, photos, letterman jackets, trophies, baseball cards. It was not easy to leave this place, because our house was stuffed full of memories as well as things. But leave we must, as the house was sold and our children mostly grown.

As I sat and began to read, I suddenly noticed a strange, intermittent wheezing sound. I looked around and saw nothing. What could it be? I went back to my reading, and again I heard it—like something being dragged across the floor. I finally got up and began to look, feeling almost frightened in the semidarkness. And then I saw it in the dining room—a frog, of all things! He must have gotten in through an open door as we'd been moving things in and out, and apparently he had gotten tangled up in some old dried poinsettia leaves that had fallen behind a piece of furniture after Christmas.

So much for Great Spiritual Thoughts and quiet time! I thought. Since I've been known to beg my husband to kill spiders for me, I thought about waking him. But Bill had been working so hard that I didn't have the heart to wake him. I reminded myself that I was now a grown woman, so I grabbed the dustpan and, after some maneuvering, coaxed the frog onto it and threw him outside on the deck. He shook off the leaves and hopped vigorously away. *Poor little thing, dragging those big old leaves.*

I sat down and again took out my notebook and Bible…and realized with a smile that maybe that's what God was doing for me—trying to set me free from dragging all the "stuff" around. My son Andy said, as I was agonizing over what to keep and what to throw away, "Mom, quit living in the past!" But how do you do that when the past so clearly defines who you are?

I thought of my blithe statement to people who asked why we were selling our house, "The house is to facilitate the life—we are not here to maintain the house. We feel God is calling us to simplify our lives." *Yeah, right,* I thought with some irony. *This whole process is certainly not simple.* It's much easier for us to keep hanging on to everything, adding and adding and adding...but it is not efficient, and it's not being a good steward of what God's given to us. Eventually, we have to deal with it. So here I was, trying to take inventory: *What do I have? What do I keep? What do I need for the future?*

Now that we are in our new house, which is smaller and differently designed, we see that some of our things just don't fit here. This move is helping me see the bigger picture, to take an inventory of my life as well. Perhaps you'd like to answer these questions, the ones I've been asking myself: *What "doesn't fit" in my life right now? What am I glad I did? What do I wish I'd done less of? What's worth my time and energy now? What's worth keeping, and what needs to go?*

The writer of Hebrews encourages us to "lay aside every weight...which so easily ensnares us, and...run with endurance the race that is set before us" (12:1). The rest of chapter 12 reminds us to be careful of stumbling— to pursue wholeness and peace, to deal with root causes of bitterness, and most of all, to accept His grace.

We can't run a good race when we're loaded down with things of the past—bitterness, what-ifs, fears, or regrets. Or even a longing for the "good old days." But as we take inventory, we see how essential it is to strengthen the good things: personal Bible study, honest, real fellowship with other believers—and following Jesus by being faithful to those He's placed in our lives and simply being obedient to His call.

Prayer

Lord, thank You that in this life You continually test our hearts. A time of transition is a good time to look again at our relationship with You. Show us what needs strengthening; show us what things in our lives need to be deleted, or what should be added. We freely open our hearts and lives to You and ask You to be Lord of all! In Jesus' name, amen.

"Holiness is not a state to be gained by going away from life, but by entering into it in the most vital way."

—Grace Brame, as quoted by Evelyn Underhill in
The Ways of the Spirit

Notes

Page 8: "How else but through…" from Oscar Wilde, "The Ballad of Reading Gaol" (1897).

Page 8: "The farther backward you look…" Winston Churchill, as quoted in William Strauss and Neil Howe, *The Fourth Turning* (New York: Broadway Books, 1997), p. 20.

Pages 19-20: "Praise to the Lord…" Hymn "Praise to the Lord, the Almighty," words by Joachim Neander, 1680; translated by Catherine Winkworth, 1863.

Page 53: "I'll go where you want me to go…" Hymn "I'll Go Where You Want Me to Go," words by Mary Brown, 1899.

Pages 98-99: "More about Jesus let me learn…" Hymn "More About Jesus," words by Eliza E. Hewitt, 1887.

Pages 108-109: "Jesus! what a friend…" Hymn "Jesus! What a Friend for Sinners," words by J. Wilbur Chapman, 1910.

Page 127: "Sometimes we just want…" Larry Crabb, *Connecting* (Nashville, TN: Word Publishing, 1997), p. 108.

Page 132: "O to grace…" Hymn "Come, Thou Fount of Every Blessing," words by Robert Robinson, 1758.

About the Author

Nancie Carmichael has worked side by side with her husband, Bill, first in pastoral ministry, and since 1979 in the writing and publishing realm. As an editor for *Virtue* magazine, she wrote articles, Bible studies, and the popular "Deeper Life" column.

Nancie now speaks at marriage retreats with her husband, as well as at a variety of women's conferences and retreats throughout the United States and Canada. Further, she has been involved in sponsoring conferences for women in prison for nearly two decades.

Parents to five children, Nancie and Bill also have several grandchildren. Nancie says about her speaking and writing, "My passion is simply to share out of my own life—as a wife, mother, and friend—the fact that we can trust God no matter what life throws at us. If I'm sure of anything, I know that He redeems and restores all that we place in His hands!"

For information about speaking, see
nanciecarmichael.com

Books by Nancie Carmichael

The Comforting Presence of God: Resting in His Unfailing Love for You

Desperate for God: How He Meets Us When We Pray

Lord, Bless My Child (with Bill Carmichael)

Lord, Bless This Marriage (with Bill Carmichael)

Selah: Your Moment to Stop, Think, and Step into Your Future

Your Life, God's Home: Knowing the Joy of His Presence

Other Good Harvest House Reading

10-MINUTE TIME OUTS FOR MOM
by *Grace Fox*

This gathering of insightful devotions will empower you to communicate with God throughout your day. Grace's homespun stories and Scripture-based prayers provide the inspiration and practical guidance you need as a busy mom to maintain a vital connection with God.

15 MINUTES ALONE WITH GOD
by *Emilie Barnes*

Designed to help you develop consistent devotional habits, *15 Minutes Alone with God* does more than just teach you how to organize your quiet times. It's also filled with warm, open meditations Emilie has written especially for you and other busy women, providing encouragement and direction for the day from someone who's been there.

30 DAYS THROUGH THE BIBLE
by *F. LaGard Smith*

This fast-paced tour of God's Word will rejuvenate your Bible reading for years to come. As you travel through the carefully selected portions of Scripture and the brief devotional comments that tie them together, the Bible's message will become crystal clear and settle more deeply into your heart and mind. Enjoy the panorama of Scripture and get a new grasp of the big picture: God's purpose for mankind and for your life.

DAILY IN CHRIST
by *Neil T. Anderson with Joanne Anderson*

With warmth and a sense of purpose, bestselling author Neil Anderson and his wife, Joanne, help you establish a faith rooted in the truth of God's Word—indeed, Christ Himself. Day by day you'll discover what it means to be a child of God and how that fact can powerfully impact the way you live.

HARVEST HOUSE
PUBLISHERS